Praise for the Books
of Stanley Weintraub

11 Days in December

"The tale of the worst Christmas for American soldiers since Valley Forge, as Weintraub puts it, is especially resonant with American troops in harm's way on Christmas, this time in Iraq and Afghanistan." —*National Review*

"A useful reminder that no matter how tough your holiday season may be, Christmas really can be a whole lot worse." —*The New York Times*

"Reading Stanley Weintraub's *11 Days in December* is like sitting down with an entertaining raconteur steeped in World War II's history and literature. This is a rewarding mosaic of personal stories." —*The Washington Post*

"Weintraub's use of the letters and diaries of 'lesser' soldiers enliven his account and make this a particularly poignant saga of men in war." —*Booklist*

"It's well written, concise, and makes good use of diaries, letters, and stories of ordinary soldiers in extraordinary times." —*USA Today*

"Compelling and intense." —*Nashville Scene*

"Anecdote-rich, dramatic, and accessible . . . Weintraub's chronicle of the terrible 'Bulge' Christmas of 1944 will be engaging reading for anyone interested in military history." —*Pages*

Silent Night

"A moving story of horror taking a holiday." —*People*

"Deeply moving." —*The Boston Globe*

"Weintraub has brought an obscure and bizarre incident to life with a flair that gives the reader a detailed glimpse at a unique Christmas story." —*The Seattle Times*

continued . . .

"This book brilliantly re-creates how, in the early months of World War I, a temporary peace broke out to celebrate Christmas. . . . To be reminded of this moving episode in history is a great gift." —*Chicago Tribune*

"An emotionally stirring, uplifting, yet ultimately sad story brilliantly told by a gifted writer."—*Booklist* (starred review)

"Stanley Weintraub's poignant account of the day one of the worst wars took a holiday sounds like the stuff of fiction, but it was the sort of event that fiction can only imitate. No wonder that his book reads like a novel, a true story that has the power to haunt."
—Robert Cowley, founding editor of *MHQ: The Quarterly Journal of Military History* and editor of *No End Save Victory: Perspectives on World War II*

General Washington's Christmas Farewell

"Stanley Weintraub's story of George Washington's triumphant journey from New York City to Virginia at the end of the Revolutionary War is in many ways America's first Christmas story, and his portrait of the humble leader who chose democracy over despotism is as inspiring today as it was more than two hundred years ago." —*The Dallas Morning News*

"Stanley Weintraub chronicles this journey beautifully . . . capturing, among much else, the democratic version of a triumphal procession [with] a bounty of enchanting facts and quotations from contemporary sources." —*The Wall Street Journal*

"The story of [Washington's] triumphal trip home, itself an act of nation building, is well told by historian Stanley Weintraub. It evokes the frail seedling from which the mighty American nation grew." —George Will

"Wisht somebody would tell me there's a Santa Claus."

Cartoon by Bill Mauldin appeared in the Army
publication *Stars and Stripes*. December 25, 1944.

11 DAYS IN DECEMBER

Christmas at the Bulge, 1944

STANLEY WEINTRAUB

NAL
CALIBER

NAL Caliber
Published by New American Library, a division of
Penguin Group (USA) Inc., 375 Hudson Street, New York, New York 10014, USA
Penguin Group (Canada), 90 Eglinton Avenue East, Suite 700, Toronto,
Ontario M4P 2Y3, Canada (a division of Pearson Penguin Canada Inc.)
Penguin Books Ltd., 80 Strand, London WC2R 0RL, England
Penguin Ireland, 25 St. Stephen's Green, Dublin 2, Ireland (a division of Penguin Books Ltd.)
Penguin Group (Australia), 250 Camberwell Road, Camberwell, Victoria 3124,
Australia (a division of Pearson Australia Group Pty. Ltd.)
Penguin Books India Pvt. Ltd., 11 Community Centre, Panchsheel Park,
New Delhi - 110 017, India
Penguin Group (NZ), 67 Apollo Drive, Rosedale, North Shore 0745,
Auckland, New Zealand (a division of Pearson New Zealand Ltd.)
Penguin Books (South Africa) (Pty.) Ltd., 24 Sturdee Avenue,
Rosebank, Johannesburg 2196, South Africa

Penguin Books Ltd., Registered Offices:
80 Strand, London WC2R 0RL, England

Published by NAL Caliber, an imprint of New American Library, a division of Penguin Group
(USA) Inc. This is an authorized reprint of a hardcover edition published by Free Press. For
information address Free Press, a division of Simon & Schuster, Inc., 1230 Avenue of the
Americas, New York, New York 10020.

First NAL Caliber Printing, September 2007
10   9   8   7   6   5

In memory of Nigel Nicolson,
a participant in these events, whose hand was in
my books, including this one over thirty years.

CONTENTS

Contents

"A clear, cold Christmas, lovely weather for killing Germans, which seems a bit queer, seeing whose birthday it is."

—*Lieutenant General George S. Patton*

"There was no Christmas for me this year, it will have to be postponed for another year or two. I just couldn't get that Christmas spirit, and who could when there is anything but peace and good will toward fellow men over here."

—*Staff Sergeant Bruce E. Egger*

"General Eisenhower acknowledges that the great German offensive which started on December 16 is a greater one than his own. . . . How would you like to die for Christmas?"

—*A German loudspeaker challenge across the line, overheard by troops of the 310th Infantry Regiment*

PREFACE

Sir, This is Patton talking . . . You have just got to make
up Your mind whose side You're on. You must come to
my assistance, so that I may dispatch the entire German
Army as a birthday present to your Prince of Peace. . . .

> —*from Lieutenant General George S. Patton's*
> *pre-Christmas prayer, at the chapel of the*
> *Fondation Pescatore, Luxembourg,*
> *December 23, 1944*

THOUSANDS UPON THOUSANDS OF LOFTY SNOW-LADEN
spruce that from a distance suggested a vast expanse of
Christmas trees stood in the dark, rugged forests of the
Ardennes overlapping the frontiers of Belgium, Luxembourg,
Germany, and France. Yet there was not much Christmas there
late in December 1944. The Battle of the Bulge, the most
intense fighting of World War II in the West since Normandy,
and soon the costliest and the most futile, was at its peak.

The Christmas tree, the most recognizable image of what
had become the major family-focused holiday in Europe and
America, had its likely origins just south of the Ardennes.
Napoleon's armies had brought decorated Christmas trees
from Alsatia into the duchies and principalities of Germany,

where the peasant practice took further hold. German immigrants carried the traditional tree across the Atlantic to America, where the custom spread in the 1820s, even before Clement Clarke Moore's ballad *The Night Before Christmas* established, or revived, other festive symbols. In the early 1840s, Queen Victoria's young consort, Prince Albert, further popularized the Christmas tradition beyond Germany when he brought candlelit tabletop trees to England from Saxony, and London's new illustrated magazines featured them.

A century later, the dark evergreen forests would be illuminated only by shot and shell. What there was of Christmas in the embattled countryside was remarkable for having survived at all.

In 1944, the lethal new war had reached its sixth Christmas for the Germans and the British, its fourth for the Americans. In an inhospitable terrain nearly dark in daylight, where dense, snow-covered evergreens recalled the season, there were few other vestiges of Christmas. Most troops hardly knew what calendar day they were trying to live through.

No single soldier can be said to have "saved" Christmas in the contested "Bulge" of the Ardennes. Many ordinary men did extraordinary things, and many extraordinary things happened to ordinary men. Still, one brash and theatrical general stood out, one who, as an invalided young officer at the close of the earlier world war, rushing from an army hospital to get back into the fighting before the Armistice occurred, had paused on the field to pen a poem about a dead colleague. He could always be expected to do the unexpected. As Christmas 1944 approached, at a medieval chapel near the battlefront, he knelt at the altar and asked God, as if the Almighty were merely a military colleague of superior rank, to grant a Christmas gift of proper killing weather. Although his form of worship seemed medieval, Lieutenant General George Smith Patton was an anachronism, and this was no ordinary Christmas.

My look at the Christmas war in 1944—what there was of it on both sides—is not a detailed military history of the Ardennes campaign. Tens of thousands of pages have been published about that, from close strategic analyses to vivid first-person accounts, and many more pages still remain to be drawn from attics and archives and memories. What follows is how it seemed then—a look at eleven days on a frozen World War II battlefront through the lens of Christmas.

Stanley Weintraub
Beech Hill
Newark, Delaware

11 DAYS IN DECEMBER

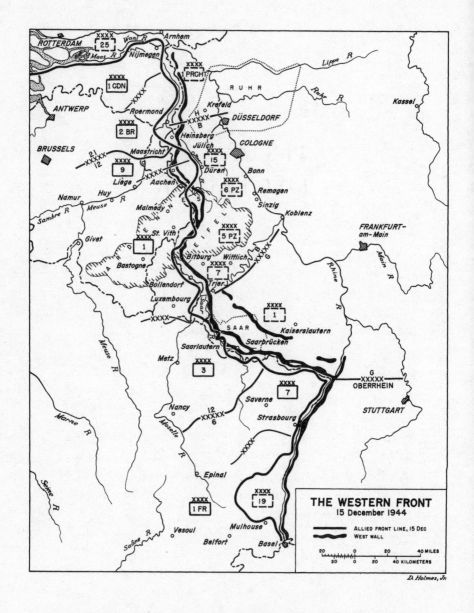

THE WESTERN FRONT
15 December 1944

ALLIED FRONT LINE, 15 DEC
WEST WALL

20   0   20   40 MILES
20   0   20   40 KILOMETERS

D. Holmes, Jr

Credit: *United States Army in World War II, The European Theater of Operations, The Ardennes: Battle of the Bulge* By Hugh M. Cole, Office of the Chief of Military History, United States Army, Washington, D.C., 1965

1

NO PEACE

Paris for Christmas! For men of the 101st Airborne Division barracked in Reims, in a camp once occupied by German infantry, the opportunity seemed alluring. Nothing appeared likely to spoil it. As *Currahee,* a postwar regimental publication, recalled, "Thru it all like a bright thread ran the anticipation of the Paris passes. Morning, noon and night, anywhere you happened to be you could hear it being discussed." Dwight D. Eisenhower, his headquarters nearby, was more avid for evenings of bridge with high-brass cronies. That a German general far on the other side of the forested line also had bridge on his mind would have surprised the Supreme Commander.

Generalfeldmarschall Hasso von Manteuffel was rethinking Hitler's risky strategy to surprise the Americans and retake the initiative long enough, at least, to forestall their expected victory in the West. "What we are planning here, General," Manteuffel explained cautiously to *Generalfeldmarschall* Walther Model, borrowing a metaphor from bridge, "is a 'grand slam' in attempting to go all the way to Antwerp. I do not think we hold the cards. I would like to see the bid reduced to a 'little slam.'" With an adversary less than alert at the holiday season, Manteuffel saw a promising, if not a decisive, hand to play.

Disguising himself as an infantry colonel, he had done some covert reconnoitering, asking returning patrols, "What are the habits of the *Amis*?" He learned that the forested Ardennes was considered "a quiet sector" by the other side, almost a rest area. Forward troops withdrew from their isolated outposts at night. Nothing much seemed to happen from darkness until dawn.

That would change in mid-December. For American soldiers, Christmas 1944 would prove the most bitter since Valley Forge. Christmas itself was almost obliterated. What happened was almost completely unanticipated. Breakthroughs into Germany and across the Rhine were in preparation, the Allies awaiting a turn in the weather. Army post-exchange officials, even more confident than frontline troops that the war with Germany would be over before the holiday season, had distributed a memorandum announcing prematurely that Christmas presents already in the European mail pipeline would be returned to the United States.

A year earlier, the Supreme Commander in the West, General Eisenhower, wagered General Bernard Law Montgomery, whose abrasive vanity he detested, £5 that Germany would surrender by Christmas 1944. Troops under Eisenhower had crossed from Sicily into the boot of Italy the month before, and Benito Mussolini's faltering government had collapsed. Arrested on the orders of his puppet king, the *Duce* had to be rescued at Hitler's instructions by an airborne commando squad led by Major Otto Skorzeny. It appeared that Germany, under enormous pressure from Russian counterattacks, and now facing a new front on the European continent in France, would gradually disintegrate.

Ike's Christmas bet of October 11, 1943, looked like a sure thing after D-Day in June 1944, when Allied forces landed across the Channel in Normandy, again under Eisenhower and once more with a British army under Montgomery, soon to be elevated to field marshal. Six weeks later, a bomb plot against Hitler by dissident officers seeking a way out of the war that would preserve Germany failed. The alleged conspirators were executed wholesale. But the *Führer* had been impaired physically and psychologically. At fifty-five he was now a bent, somewhat deaf, yet intense old man with tremors and a lame arm he tried to conceal.

Allied and Soviet armies now pressed on toward the German heartland. On October 23, American chief of staff General George C. Marshall cabled Eisenhower urging that "an immediate supreme effort . . . may well result in the collapse of German resistance before the heavy winter weather limits large operations and facilitates [enemy] defensive strategy." He offered "maximum support for this all-out effort," which might "contribute to defeating Germany by 1 January 1945." A copy went to British chief of staff Sir Alan Brooke, who noted in his diary his own hope that Germany might be finished off by the end of the year.

Closer to the action, the imminent implosion of the *Reich* was so taken for granted that Eisenhower's commanders hesitated absorbing unnecessary casualties. Yet in the fog, rain and mud of late autumn their advance, bogged down besides by their gasoline and ammunition shortages, had slowed to a near stalemate. Channel ports could not cope with the massive appetites of armies in the field, especially for fuel. Enduring an icy Ardennes or *Hürtgenwald* winter now seemed hardship enough for troops without the added hazards of shot and shell. More men than any headquarters would acknowledge opted out of the war, often vanishing without leave into the ferment of Belgium and France. Commitment to a quick victory soon flagged.

The waning of Allied momentum proved more costly than anticipated. In the Hürtgen Forest, southeast of Aachen (a city that itself took weeks to seize despite the dogged defenders in some units being the scrap heap of the *Wehrmacht*), an American officer confided, "We are taking three trees a day, yet they cost us about 100 men apiece." The Germans even booby-trapped the bodies of their own dead, making the instinctive hunt for service souvenirs alarmingly hazardous.

Eisenhower's strategy of pressing the war on all fronts rather than holding a broad line and investing resources in a single powerful strike into Germany—Montgomery's contrary obsession, provided he commanded the operation—had thinned the margins of military superiority. Exhausted divisions had little opportunity to rest and refit, except in supposedly quiet, road-poor, fog-blanketed areas—like the Ardennes and the forest of the Eifel. With their rehabilitation now a priority, General Marshall had slowed sending divisions to the Pacific for the invasion of Japan. The long process of drafting and training and transporting new recruits might take a year or more.

As crossing the Rhine now seemed to be a matter for a post-winter campaign, Winston Churchill deplored what he imagined as lost opportunities, privately blaming Eisenhower rather than the September failures of his favorite, Montgomery. To Jan Smuts in South Africa, the British prime minister cabled on December 3, 1944, "Eisenhower has of course sustained a strategic reverse. . . . Before the offensive was launched we placed on record our view that it was a mistake to attack against the whole front and that a far greater mass should have been gathered at the point of desired penetration. Montgomery's comments and predictions beforehand have been borne out." Although he would never criticize Monty, when Churchill edited the cable for publication in his memoirs in 1953, he quietly changed "Eisenhower has . . ." to "We have . . ." Nevertheless, the strategic reverse in the Ardennes would be compounded in spades two weeks after the cable to Smuts.

Despite the earlier optimism in Washington and London, Christmas would arrive before Germany collapsed. Yet the end, however delayed, still seemed clear from Hitler's desperate resort to new improvised *Volkssturm* divisions—teenage troops and overage reserves from sixteen (often fourteen) to sixty. Allied forces, despite shortages of antifreeze and winterized boots, were now bestride the frontiers of Germany itself and had reoccupied much of Belgium and Luxembourg. But Eisenhower, also running short in reserves, had to curtail his progress. The pause bought the Germans time.

On December 19, Major Tom Bigland, a liaison officer deputed by Montgomery to the headquarters of Lieutenant General Courtney Hodges of the American First Army in Spa, found neither Hodges nor any of his staff. Bigland did not know that a panicky report received by Hodges at 4:00 p.m. the previous day had claimed that an entire German panzer division was heading toward them. "General," Colonel William Sylvan, who had come in to warn Hodges, said in puzzlement, "some of our tanks are a mile down the road firing in this direction."

Attuned, or so he thought, to sound identifications, Hodges looked up and said, "Bill, those aren't our tanks; those are German tanks." He went back to his papers, but then realized what he had said. Soon a Piper Cub was waiting at Maroon

Airstrip to take him out of trouble. His staff fled the venerable Hôtel Britannique, in the historic Belgian resort town from which Kaiser Wilhelm in November 1918 had abdicated his throne and escaped to Holland. Hastily packing or burning files, they abandoned their offices and hurried by road through the early winter darkness to Chaudfontaine, the First Army rear command post near Liège.

According to Sylvan, "By one of the fortunes of war that cannot be explained, the [German] tanks turned southwest from La Gleize, and reports that they were a mile away from the outskirts of Spa proved untrue." Still, there remained cause for alarm. "A buzz bomb going down the alley toward Liège . . . hit a truck of G-4 [Supply] killing all 14 occupants. What was left of the 2½ ton truck was a small crumpled mass that was thrown in the river. . . . At midnight we pulled into the new CP . . . , the second floor of the Palace Hotel."

According to the astonished Bigland, the next afternoon he "found no Army M.P.s in Spa and walked into the [Hodges] H.Q. to find literally *not one single person* there except a German [cleaning] woman. Breakfast was laid and the Christmas tree was decorated in the dining room, telephones were in all the offices, papers were all over the place—but there was no one there to tell visitors where they had gone to! Germans in the town said that they had gone suddenly and quickly down the road. . . . I found them again at their rear H.Q. and here they had even less control of the battle than the day before."* As

---

*According to Colonel Charles C. Patterson in 1973, "All my officers and men had received their Christmas presents, which hadn't been opened, so they were all loaded into the trailer that went [to Liège] with my van. . . . But I maintained an advance headquarters in Spa. That was the way I was in constant communication." If so, he was well concealed from friend as well as foe. He also recalled a V-1 bomb interrupting Christmas dinner at "the Colonel's mess" in Liège.

"LO" he reported his shocking findings to a displeased Montgomery.

Hearing that an SS *Kampfgruppe* was heading for Spa, the mayor, playing both sides, released twenty alleged German collaborators from jail, while other local officials prudently removed from the walls of the town hall portraits of Churchill and Roosevelt, and American, British, and Belgian flags. No enemy combatants ever came. Spa was bypassed.

In another Belgian town where Americans had billeted, and Major William Desobry, commander of the 20th Armored Infantry Battalion, encountered a thick morning fog, the expected Germans in halftracks with 88-mm guns had not yet appeared. "You could see," he wrote, "an American unit had been there, abandoned all their stuff, their bedding, their bunks, and had written on the wall, 'We shall return,' like MacArthur." Desobry would soon become a prisoner of war.

Less than a week earlier, a British liaison officer at Eisenhower's domain in Versailles, Lieutenant Colonel David Niven, better known on the Hollywood screen, was at First Army headquarters to visit an old friend, Captain Bob Low. A former reporter for *Time*, Low had become an intelligence officer. He showed Niven the map room of the G-2 [Intelligence] section. "What happens here?" Niven asked.

"You mean here in Spa?" Low pointed out the window to the east. "You see the trees on the top of those hills? Well, on the other side of those hills, there is a forest, and in that forest they are now forming the Sixth Panzer Army and any day now the Sixth Panzer Army is going to come right through this room and out the other side, cross the Meuse, then swing right and go north to Antwerp." Teeming Antwerp was now the crucial harbor servicing Eisenhower's armies, and by Low's educated guess, Hitler's goal.

"Have you told anyone?" Niven, in what may have been a somewhat embellished recollection, laughed at the fantasy forecast.

"We've been telling them for days," Low said. "Every day we have to give them three appreciations [estimates] of what we *think* may happen. That has been our number-one appreciation."

The next day, Niven recalled, "I went down through the fog-shrouded Forest of Ardennes to Marche [-en-Famenne, southwest of Spa]. Within hours the last great German offensive of the war erupted."

The Sixth Panzers foreseen by Low were a tough bunch with the best equipment available, commanded by SS General "Sepp" Dietrich, once a butcher, and a crony of the *Führer* since the failed Beer Hall Putsch of 1923. While some generals proclaimed confidence in what was described as a sacred mission, Dietrich no longer harbored illusions about their prospects, unlike passionate younger Nazis. Zealously, a junior officer in the 12th SS Panzer Division wrote home, "Some believe in living, but life is not everything! It is enough to know that we attack, and we will throw the enemy from our homeland. It is a holy task."

Bob Low's G-2 boss, Colonel Benjamin ("Monk") Dickson, had also identified potential danger over the hills, although Hodges himself saw no opportunities for enemy armor in that roads-poor terrain. Dickson in any case was on Christmas leave in Paris, his very absence for the holidays suggesting the low level of anxiety in Spa.

Despite the evidence of Hodges's abandoned Christmas tree, as early as the sixteenth, the likelihood of even vestiges of a traditional holiday up and down the line had begun to evaporate. Yet with no warning from his own intelligence sources to alter his plans, Montgomery had requested formal permission from Eisenhower the day before to return to England to spend the school Christmas holiday with his son, David, then sixteen. (His mother, Monty's wife, Betty, had died in 1937.) With the message, Montgomery enclosed without comment Eisenhower's signed memorandum dated from Italy, "Amount £5. Eisenhower bets war with Germany will end before Xmas 1944—local time." Monty's lack of confidence was not misplaced. He had contributed substantially to the delays from D-Day onward. From the beginning of November into mid-December his own forces had advanced just ten miles.

Agreeing that there was no military urgency to keep Montgomery from visiting his son, Eisenhower conceded, "I still have nine days, and while it seems almost certain that you will have an extra five pounds for Christmas, you will not get it until that day. At least you must admit we have gone a long ways toward the defeat of Germany since we made our bet. . . ." Then he penned Christmas greetings to Field Marshal Alan Brooke, Admiral Andrew Cunningham, Winston Churchill's military aide General "Pug" Ismay, and Churchill himself.

Secret "Ultra" decrypts from relevant German communications had been sparse and seemingly insignificant. Yet when "Ultra" revealed *Luftwaffe* aircraft reinforcements gathering near the Rhine, and *Reichsbahn* troop trains bringing newly organized divisions west, Allied intelligence saw nothing extraordinary. Eisenhower's staff also knew of Hitler's boasts to Baron Hiroshi Oshima, the Japanese ambassador, intercepted as usual from radiograms, of a counteroffensive to come, to obstruct the breaching of his last homeland defenses.

Eisenhower had last made a tour of the lines from November 8 through November 11. An army photo shows him at

Major General Troy Middleton's forward post at Wiltz in Luxembourg, southeast of Bastogne. With him are Middleton; Lieutenant General Omar Bradley, with a revolver slung under his left armpit; and Major General John Leonard of the 9th Armored Division. Eisenhower is perched on a battered desk, coffee in a chipped cup in one hand, in the other a cigarette from the three packs he smoked through every day.

His report to Marshall on the day before he returned to Versailles began, with exculpatory exasperation, "I am getting exceedingly tired of [the] weather." He reported "floods in Patton's area," caused by heavy rains which deprived him of air support. "Then the floods came down the [Moselle] river, [a mile wide at one point], and not only washed out two fixed bridges, but destroyed his principal floating bridge and made others almost unusable." Nevertheless, Ike assured Marshall, "We will get ahead all along his [Patton's] front." And Patton did advance, briefly, encircling Metz on November 18 and capturing it four days later, the first time that the fortress city had fallen to an enemy since AD 415. With a flair for self-promotion, Patton ensured that the soldier-correspondents of *Yank* and *Stars and Stripes* knew all the details of his Third Army successes.

Eisenhower also reported that he and Bradley had visited every division in Hodges's First and Simpson's Ninth Armies, finding GI morale (probably put on for his inspection) "surprisingly high" and troops "rather comfortable," with "no signs of exhaustion." In the hills, snow had already reached six inches, but lower down, the snow still "melted rather rapidly" (which also meant morasses of mud). It was then still early November, and Marshall's own war experience in the region in 1918 must have caused him to wonder about what further progress could be expected when real winter came. The Germans were receiving weather data from remote outposts* on the North Atlantic and from briefly surfaced submarines, and were counting on continued forecasts of poor skies. "All of us keep hoping," Eisenhower disclosed to Marshall, attempting to appear upbeat, "that some little spell will come along in which we can have a bit of relief from mud, rain and fog so that tanks and infantry can operate more easily on the offensive and so that we can use our great air asset. In spite of difficulties, no one is discouraged and we will yet make the German wish that he had gone completely back of the Rhine at the end of his great retreat across France."

The strategic situation still did not seem particularly worrisome when Eisenhower cabled Marshall's logistics chief in Washington, Lieutenant General Brehon Somervell, a month later that the Germans had launched "a rather ambitious counterattack east of the Luxembourg area where we have been holding rather thinly." Such forested and riverine areas seemed unlikely to sustain serious troop movements or offer surfaces for armor, and Eisenhower had concentrated his forces, he explained to Somervell, at more "vital points." Shrugging off the gross intelligence failures, he was "closing in on the new threats from each flank. If things go well we should not only stop the thrust but should be able to profit from it."

Things did not go well. When the temperature was not cold enough for snow, the incessant rain and overcast skies prevented air support of operations. Hitler counted on it. His solution, planned once he had recovered enough from the July bomb, was to consult the ultimate authority in the Third Reich, his own intuition. It wasn't always wrong.

---

*Weather stations on the east coast of Greenland and the Norwegian island of Spitsbergen.

Although the Allied advance in early autumn seemed unstoppable, Hitler hoped to put Germany in a position to broker a deal with Russia, or with the West, or both. From Baron Hiroshi Oshima, who had been a solicitous well-wisher during Hitler's weeks of recovery from the attempt on his life, he had learned of Japan's continued attempts to bribe Russia into keeping the peace in Asia. Hitler could no longer tempt Stalin into a deal in Europe to keep the West from dominating Germany to Soviet disadvantage; it seemed too late for that. Yet putting the Reich's remaining resources into denying the Anglo-Americans victory might buy time to further develop "miracle" weapons. The first twenty-five supersonic, if erratic, V-2 rockets, launched into the stratosphere in early September, were a frightening beginning. There was no defense against them. Thousands more were being manufactured by brutal exploitation of slave labor. The new "*schnorkel*" submarines, capable of long undersea operations, were another weapon going into production. Allied attrition and defeat might also encourage Western anti-Communism, creating a desire for accommodation with Germany to keep the Soviets away. Hitler's counteroffensive, however, had to succeed *before* the Russians penetrated Germany from Poland—which meant during the late-autumn and winter months of overcast and icy weather that could nullify Allied air supremacy while keeping Red Army air and armor at bay.

When still bedridden from his injuries in late September, Hitler had called in General Alfred Jodl to review with him maps of the Ardennes, the area lightly manned by the Americans even though the Germans had exploited its terrain in 1940 to blitz the French. Despite recent history, it did seem a natural barrier to armor. Thrusting through the forest of the Ardennes to reach the Meuse to the west to retake Antwerp, 125 miles to the north, would require hoarding scarce fuel for tracked vehicles that used it up at a ravenous half-gallon per mile. After the first few days, panzer divisions would have to seize enemy gasoline storage facilities. Success at both goals presumably would demoralize the West while bottling up resupply of its troops.

In mid-October, to defuse a coup in Budapest that could take Hungary out of the war, Hitler had ordered Major Otto Skorzeny—who had snatched Mussolini from Italian partisans—to kidnap the son of Hungarian dictator Admiral Nikolaus Horthy. When Skorzeny arrived at Hitler's bunker in East Prussia, soon to be evacuated ahead of the Red Army, to report success, the *Führer* raised him to the SS equivalent of lieutenant colonel and said, "Don't go, Skorzeny, I have perhaps the most important job in your life for you. So far very few people know of the preparations for a secret plan in which you have an important part to play. In December, Germany will start a great offensive, which may well decide her fate." Skorzeny was to create disarray as the Ardennes breakout began by leading commandos disguised in American uniforms, fluent in American idiom, and using vehicles with American markings. To give the plan a cover of unreality his Panzer Brigade 150, authorized at 3,300 men, would be code-named *Greif*. (The fabled Griffin has the head and wings of an eagle and a lion's body.)

When on October 26 Skorzeny received a copy of a printed notice being distributed across the Western Front, headed "Secret Commando Operations," he was baffled. "The *Führer*," it began, "has ordered the formation of a special unit of approximately two-battalion strength for use on the Western Front in special operations." English-speaking men from all services were invited to volunteer for *Dienstelle Skorzeny* and report for training to an "American School" near the Rhine on November 10. Skorzeny urgently contacted Hitler's headquarters to ask that the action be abandoned, as the open distribution of the notice gave his mission away to Allied intelligence. Hitler conceded that the mistake was unfortunate, but thought it might escape notice by the enemy. It did not—but Allied intelligence scorned it as disinformation. Skorzeny was too notorious.

Earlier in October, Jodl had presented Hitler with a draft of plans for a pre-Christmas offensive that he called, perhaps deliberately suggesting a different season, "Christrose." It banked on the unforeseen, and on bad weather, for a breakthrough to Antwerp in seven days. The code name would be changed, and changed again. "Watch on the Rhine," soon renamed "Autumn Mist," was approved by Hitler on October 9. Details were confirmed for German commanders by Jodl on November 3. Half of the sixteen divisions would be armored. The footsoldiers would largely be cobbled-together replacements, many from now-surplus *Kriegsmarine* and *Luftwaffe* ranks, augmented by conscripts from factory jobs and regiments waiting out the winter in Italy. When ready, they would sweep through the thinnest Allied lines to create panic.

Although the Germans would muster initially about 200,000 troops and 800 tanks against an expected 80,000 Americans in the Ardennes with 600 tanks, no one in the *Wehrmacht* command thought the forces were adequate for extended winter warfare, nor that reaching distant Antwerp was realistic. The *Amis* could rush in reinforcements by the thousands. (Eventually 600,000 GIs would be involved.) The Germans would have no recourse to replacements other than units transferred from distant or noncombat assignments. Jodl reminded the generals nevertheless that timidity was not an option. Limited gains would not suffice "to make the western powers ready to negotiate."

Hitler signed final orders on November 10. Delays in organizing troops and equipment moved the start to December 16. To keep tight control of operations, he left Berlin secretly on December 10 to establish headquarters in bunkers built for him at Ziegenberg, site of a medieval castle near Bad Nauheim. The next day, at what Hitler christened *Adlerhorst* (Eagle's Nest), holding his unusable arm behind him, he spoke to a gathering of top officers about his intentions. "Wars are finally decided," Hitler argued, "through the recognition by one side or the other that the war as such can no longer be won. To get the enemy to realize this is therefore the most important task."

Unconditional surrender had been an Allied demand to offset Stalin's paranoia about a deceitful separate peace. Hitler ruled surrender out. "Let no moment pass," he insisted, "without making plain to the enemy that whatever he does he can never reckon with [our] capitulation, never, never." Although Christmas was only two weeks away, he did not wish the high brass, in closing, a *"fröliche Weihnachten."* He assumed there would be none.

2

CHRISTMAS GIFTS

O N December 15, First Army intelligence picked up a signal that the *Reichswehr* intended to recapture Aachen, on the border, as a Christmas present for the *Führer*. It suggested, if not strategic fakery, a very limited offensive to retrieve the only German city then lost to the Allies. Few in Eisenhower's headquarters in Versailles took it seriously.

On December 16, the top brass in the American military worldwide, however distracted by immediate concerns, received its own early Christmas gifts. On the same day that Eisenhower sent holiday greetings to the likes of Winston Churchill, Hastings Ismay, and Alan Brooke, Congress passed, and the president signed, legislation advancing to five-star rank seven senior officers. Marshall had long deplored the bill as unnecessary, and some newspapers had speculated that the rank of field marshal, used elsewhere, would have created in his case the anomaly of *Marshal Marshall*. "I didn't want any promotion at all," he told historian and wartime sergeant Forrest Pogue in 1956. "I didn't need it. . . . I didn't want to be beholden to Congress for any rank or anything of that kind. I wanted to be able to go in there with my skirts clean and no personal ambition . . . , and I could get all I wanted with the rank I had. But that was twisted around and somebody said I didn't like the term *marshal* because it was the same as my name. I know Mr. Churchill twitted me about this."

Marshall also thought that the idea of parity of rank with other armies was useless. British field marshals were already senior to him by date of appointment, and the Soviets already used six stars for super-ranks. The navy had been pushing for five stars since November 1942, and under pressure from President Franklin D. Roosevelt and Secretary of War Henry Stimson, Marshall finally compromised on "General of the Army," with the navy equivalent of "Fleet Admiral." Advanced in order of seniority were William D. Leahy, George C. Marshall, Ernest J. King, Douglas MacArthur, Chester W. Nimitz, Dwight D. Eisenhower, and Henry H. ("Hap") Arnold.

MacArthur's date of rank would precede Ike's by two days. Pleased with the stars and relieved that he would outrank Eisenhower, his one-time aide, if only fractionally, MacArthur rushed a saccharine radiogram to President Roosevelt, whom he despised: "My grateful thanks for the promotion you have just given me. My pleasure in receiving it is greatly enhanced because it was made by you." Too impatient in Leyte to wait for official insignia, he had a circlet of five small stars crafted for him by a Filipino silversmith in Tacloban, using, he claimed, metal from American, Australian, Dutch, and Philippine coins to symbolize the national elements of his command. On the day after Christmas his handmade insignia was ready. Two of MacArthur's generals, for the cameras, ceremoniously pinned the circlets on his lapels.

Marshall, by contrast, wrote a laconic two-sentence appreciation of the president's "confidence" in him. Eisenhower only cabled Marshall asking him to thank the president "for the continued confidence in me and in this command." He was occupied on the Saturday morning of the sixteenth by the wedding of his valet Sergeant Mickey McKeough to WAC corporal Pearlie Hargrave in the Louis XIV Chapel in Versailles, then in having the Supreme Headquarters staff toast his elevation to five stars with champagne. It seemed a good war.

More concrete faith in Eisenhower came from Marshall, Roosevelt, and Stimson. However dismayed by sudden news of a turnabout in the Ardennes, they intended to leave Eisenhower free from nagging by Washington. "I shall merely say now that you have our complete confidence," Marshall cabled. On December 22 he added, "I am sorry that your Christmas Day must be one of storm and stress." He "kept down" all messages to Eisenhower, even recalling one from the Pentagon before it was transmitted, advising his staff, "Don't bother him." The attitude of the White House especially pleased Marshall. "Roosevelt didn't send a word to Eisenhower nor ask [him] a question. In great stress Roosevelt was a strong man."

There also was a war going on across the world from the Ardennes. MacArthur's divisions in Leyte were pushing the Japanese farther into the northwest hills of the island. The invasion begun on October 20 had not been expected to extend—as it did—into Christmas and beyond. Mindoro was to be next, and then Luzon. Tacloban, the Leyte capital, and its airfield, had long been in American hands, and MacArthur had taken over the elegant, stucco enemy officers' club (once the home of a wealthy American the Japanese had conveniently killed) as his headquarters. From there he let Generals Walter Krueger and

Robert Eichelberger run the war while he smoked his corncob pipe on the veranda, watched movies in the evening, turned civil administration over to the rather reluctant President Sergio Osmeña (who had succeeded to the office-in-exile on the death of Manuel Quezon), wrote communiqués for his publicists to distribute as if their own, and entertained visiting correspondents and dignitaries.

MacArthur's Christmas Eve in Leyte would be an improvement on Eisenhower's. Although Jean and little Arthur remained in Brisbane, the general expected to import them to Luzon once he retook Manila. His pacing alone after dark, reminiscent of his Manila Hotel days before the war, was less quiet than usual as a GI group gathered below to sing carols in a steamy locale that hardly resembled a traditional American Christmas setting. As he paused to listen, several Japanese nuisance raiders in low-flying planes buzzed the compound. The singing stopped abruptly and the soldiers sought cover in the hedges. Searchlights caught one of the intruders in their crossbeams and a burst of antiaircraft fire shot it down. MacArthur thanked the carolers and resumed his pacing.

When the Germans struck, Marshall had been busy rethinking post-Europe assignments for MacArthur to the Pacific, and new roles for airborne divisions. Major General Matthew B. Ridgway, commander of the recently created Eighteenth Airborne Corps, had sent Major General Maxwell D. Taylor, who led the 101st Airborne Division, to Washington to promote more effective use of what the War Department conceived of as small combat groups that deployed only by parachute or glider. To retain that distinction they were often underutilized. Ridgway wanted them available "to fight on the line . . . when not being employed as an Airborne Unit." In a message to Marshall in September 1943, after the invasion of Sicily, Eisenhower said flatly, "I do not believe in the airborne division." (He never would.) "Just now," Marshall (on December 18) would have to cable Ridgway about further discussions, "it would appear that you could not leave the theater. In January the situation should be much clearer. . . . The courage and dash of airborne troops has become a by-word and is a great inspiration to all the others." And he closed, "With warm regards and the hope that you find some cheer in the Christmas season. . . ."

Courage and dash were already called for, and the need for chutists fighting on the line had emerged urgently by the time Ridgway read Marshall's message in England. Ridgway and Taylor were the only significant Allied commanders with troops across the Channel who were not on the scene in mid-December. Some generals had been comparatively relaxed, ready to wait out the winter. The Rhine would still be there when its surface ice thawed.

Intending to go home for Christmas and convinced that the Germans "cannot stage offensive operations," Montgomery still retired every evening at 9:30. Hodges in Spa had put up his Christmas tree. So had Monty, who also tacked his Christmas cards on the wall.

On the southern edge of what was being lightly called a Ghost Front, Bradley before leaving for Paris had put up at the comfortable Hotel Alfa in Luxembourg City, the somnolent capital of the duchy. At Versailles he would ask Eisenhower for infantry replacements from swollen rear-area units. In his own bloated headquarters in a city famous for its hotels, Bradley, a commander in parallel to Monty, employed nearly five thousand support personnel who had no expectation of ever firing a weapon.

Eisenhower had flown to Maastricht in southern Holland to meet Montgomery and Bradley early in December to discuss how to reactivate the dormant war. From London, Field Marshal Brooke, Monty's most passionate promoter, saw no quick end in sight. Not long before he had complained to his diary about "the very unsatisfactory state of affairs in France, with no one running the land battle." Since Montgomery's embarrassment at Arnhem in September, when his airborne attack failed, and Allied troops had to retreat from the Rhine with heavy casualties, he had lain low. Brooke had been scheming with him "to counter the pernicious American strategy of attacking all along the line" by "splitting an army group with the Ardennes in the middle of it." By dividing Bradley's forces, the ambitious Monty would gain control of the entire ground war, to strike on his own toward Berlin. Lodged near Paris, Eisenhower seemed to him aloof and distant and overly cautious. From deep in the Ardennes the Germans would inadvertently assist Monty's ambitions.

A diary entry by Brooke also charged Eisenhower, very likely from gossip passed on by Montgomery, with failing to take charge. "Ike," Brooke had written on November 24, "does not hope to cross the Rhine before May!!!" Rather, the general was "by himself with his lady chauffeur [, Kay Summersby,] on the golf links at Rheims*—entirely detached from the war and taking practically no part in the running of the war! Matters got so bad lately that a deputation of [Major General John] Whiteley, Bedell Smith, and a few others went up to tell him that he must get down to it and RUN the war, which he said he would. Personally I think he is incapable of running the war even if he tries."† Smith himself, Eisenhower's

---

*The British still spelled Reims with an added *h*.

†When historian Arthur Bryant published an edition of the last years of Brooke's diaries in 1959 as *Triumph in the West*, he cut the last sentence, but even so the words he left caused widespread outrage in the U.S. Eisenhower was then in the White House.

chief of staff, Brooke added, lived in a posh Paris hotel amid a huge Supreme Headquarters entourage, content to leave the war "in a rudderless condition." Lieutenant General J.C.H. Lee's sprawling and sluggish COM-Z (Communications Zone) logistics empire in Paris was even more swollen, with 29,000 Services of Supply troops enjoying the city. Lee himself lived in imperial style.

In November, American divisions had already taken heavy losses in the hilly and densely wooded *Hürtgenwald,* just inside the German border. Air support there seemed useless. Farther east were the *Schnee Eifel* (Snow Mountains), wooded hills, and rushing streams, in which eighteenth-century villages nestled in the valleys. Eight miles deep by twenty miles wide, the Hürtgen had cost 25,000 American casualties in October and November. The broader Ardennes, overlapping France and southern Belgium and extending to the meandering Meuse and Aisne rivers, was 2,015 square miles of rugged forest, miserable in rain, mud, and sleet. There, German *Kampfgruppen* were assembling to little Allied notice.

Since communications up and down the line were poor, Bradley had little picture of the status of the front. Bad weather kept activity minimal. By December 15 the Germans had unloaded in the *Schnee Eifel* area 1,502 troop trains and nearly 500 supply trains. American intelligence was unaware of anything unusual. By early afternoon on the 16th, one of Bradley's aides in Luxembourg City already had a copy, taken from a prisoner, of Field Marshal Gerd von Rundstedt's Order of the Day, too late to matter. It was not a deception, although disinformation was often planted that way. The message exuded an Hitlerian faith, in which Rundstedt did not believe, referring to the "holy obligation to give everything to achieve things beyond human possibilities for our Fatherland and *Führer.*"

Hasso von Manteuffel's Order of the Day exhorted more succinctly, "Forward double time."

Radio intercepts failed to reveal offensive preparations. The Germans were careful, and few reconnaissance aircraft had been able to fly. Fake German signals indicated only normal defensive activity, except for some suggestions that a counteroffensive might be launched to deter an expected British thrust toward Cologne and the Ruhr industrial area. However, Colonel Monk Dickson's intelligence crew had estimated to General Hodges as early as December 9, based on prisoner interrogations, that the Sixth Panzer Army opposite Bradley's 12th Army Group was preparing an attack. Hodges remained skeptical that it meant anything. So did Eisenhower's headquarters. Nothing would happen before Christmas. Since generals knew better, Dickson applied for Christmas leave in Paris.

Without leave, many soldiers had already gone on holiday. Rather than fight in wintry conditions, or at all, tens of thousands of GI deserters were vanishing into French cities, brazenly living on stolen rations and trafficking in black market military goods, even hijacking vehicles. Nearly two thousand, many of them officers, were already in prisoner cages in Paris, charged with "misappropriation." Although the equivalent of two divisions, the culprits were quietly unnoticed by newspapermen, who wanted to keep their accreditation. (The British estimated that their own AWOL personnel, also deep into criminality and unreported in print, would populate a further division.) Eisenhower would describe the situation as "unconscionable thievery and racketeering"—yet by June 1945, citing an administrative backlog, he intervened to reduce most sentences or suspend them altogether. There were precedents. Lincoln had done much the same with deserting Union troops.

Signs of a pending attack continued to surface, and commanders continued to ignore them. In the U.S., General Peyton C. March, the World War I chief of staff and, at eighty, long retired, would tell a *New York Times* interviewer that when he heard excuses about bad weather and unmanageable surfaces, "I just fall on my knees and weep. . . . Imagine the population of Richmond, Virginia, being assembled across the Potomac and we not knowing about it!"

In the hilly Belgian crossroads town of Bastogne, Troy Middleton, whose VIII Corps' front straddled eighty miles of the Ardennes on the west, was informed on December 15 about a peasant woman sent by the 28th Division who claimed to have seen, before slipping away from a work party, German troops and tanks massing east of Clervaux, twenty miles away. Elise Delé-Dunkel had observed horse-drawn wagons laden with pontoons and small boats, and troops in SS uniforms, and overheard soldiers talking about their three weeks' struggle to get there from Italy. Much too slowly, her warnings worked their way to higher command.

Routine patrolling had been minimal in the poor weather and treacherous terrain, especially after dark. No unusual activity had been detected. In the nine-to-five war the arrivals of troop trains were downplayed as rotating replacements. Yet the carriages returning from the Westwall, the series of bunkers and natural barriers that largely followed the prewar border with Belgium, Luxembourg, and France, were empty. From the German standpoint there was no border with Luxembourg. The 999-square-mile German-speaking duchy had been incorporated into the *Reich* after the blitzkreig in 1940, and once the counterattack from the east came, nervous Luxembourgers, like some Belgians, discreetly removed their Allied flags.

Since a First Army interrogator assumed that boats and

bridging equipment suggested offensive action, Frau Delé-Dunkel had been escorted up the red-tape chain to the headquarters of General Hodges in Spa, whose intelligence chief was on leave in Paris. She was listened to politely and sent home. A scouting party from the inexperienced 106th "Golden Lion" Division had earlier captured two enemy footsoldiers in the Ardennes. Unseasoned POWs were the best information sources. They confessed that fresh troops were arriving and that an attack was coming perhaps in a day or two, certainly by Christmas. Intelligence assumed the usual disinformation expected from prisoners. Civilian claims were also suspect, as the region housed German sympathizers and resettled Germans. Some Belgian border areas had been loyal to Leon Degrelle's homegrown Fascist movement with Hitler Youth units and a regiment of local volunteers to fight the Russians. A leading Luxembourg Nazi who had slipped away to Germany was broadcasting defiance nightly from a radio station in Trier, thirty-two miles eastward.

A rumor was checked out that residents were placing color-coded cloth panels in the fields to mark enemy parachute-drop zones. None were found; the report was dismissed as disinformation to sow panic. A Polish conscript in the SS who was captured after he was injured setting a mine, told of railheads beyond the *Westwall* defenses in towns like Bitburg, where fresh troops were arriving daily and being sent into the *Schnee Eifel*. Taking the prisoner seriously, an intelligence officer jeeped to the command post of Major General Alan Jones, of the 106th Division in St. Vith, a town on the edge of the German lines. One of the railheads identified by the Pole was Losheim, just above St. Vith.

The clamor of massing motors and the clanking of tracked vehicles was muffled by the forest and by the deliberate droning of German aircraft. So many columns of tanks and towed artillery had lined up in the darkness that carefully hoarded fuel was wasted as engines idled. It was often too cold not to keep them running. Propagandized to a high pitch of intensity, *Panzergrenadiers* expected the offensive to be the last roll of the strategic dice to win in the West. One would write on a wall as he broke into Luxembourg, "*Hinter der letzen Schlacht dieser Kriege esteht unser Sieg!*" The last word was in bold lettering five times the size of the rest: "Behind the last battle of this war stands our VICTORY!"

3

BREAKTHROUGH

A T 5:30 A.M. ON DECEMBER 16, TROOPS ON THE Ardennes front awakened to the flash and roar of German artillery, from mortars and howitzers to distant railway guns rifling fourteen-inch shells. Few surface telephone lines survived, and American radio was jammed as the Germans played phonograph records loudly on known military frequencies. After an hour the artillery fell silent, and while searchlights, casting ghostly reflections landward, probed toward the clouds in the pre-dawn drizzle and fog, white-clad forms moved toward the dazed Americans. Some fled; other platoons were overrun; a few companies held to their positions and returned fire. Few had dug in defensively, and the front was too sparsely held to maintain a firm line. Enemy infantrymen slipped through seams between strongpoints. When Bruce Clarke arrived at the disarray of Alan Jones's 106th Division command post near St. Vith early on Sunday, December 17, General Jones confessed wearily, "I have no division. . . . I have two regiments out on the Schnee Eifel, and my son is in one of them."

Refitted and mostly veteran panzer and *volksgrenadier* divisions from the Eastern Front, once identified as such from prisoners taken, made it clear that Omar Bradley's divisions were not facing what he first dismissed as "just a goddam little spoiling attack." Major General Leonard Gerow of V Corps to the north took what was happening more seriously. At eleven on the morning of the sixteenth he had telephoned Hodges in Spa, appealing, "I'd like to halt my attack." An offensive being readied was in trouble. Gerow needed to reassemble troops knocked off the line. "Keep your attack moving," the poorly informed Hodges insisted. Although the Germans had massed forces to push toward the Meuse, as planned, and then probe northward toward Antwerp, the realization that more than a local counterattack was in progress had not yet sunk in. From Versailles, Eisenhower had just sent off his message to Montgomery that he had nine days left to win his Christmas wager. Not yet having flown home to visit his son, Monty was off playing golf. His segment of Holland was quiet.

Out of touch with events on the line, Bradley had left by staff car for Versailles to consult with Eisenhower about replacements. Attrition had reduced most of his divisions below authorized levels. Rifle companies were especially ragged, and men transferred from other services and distant from their basic training were proving unsatisfactory, drawing high casualties.

Driven about in his lumbering armored Cadillac, Bradley had been escorting actress Marlene Dietrich to USO appearances anticipating the Christmas season. American troops were enthusiastically appreciative. In lieu of autographs, she furnished lipstick kisses—on paper—to GIs who crowded around her. Two weeks short of forty-three, Miss Dietrich had aged almost unnoticeably. Traveling down the front from Maastricht to Nancy, she wore "long, wooly drop-seat underwear" under a khaki uniform that exuded her glamor, and a knitted khaki helmet liner tilted suggestively askew, one swirl of lacquered blond hair above her forehead. In performance she often switched, whatever the temperature and platform, to nylons and a sequined evening gown that warmed her audiences, most of them half her years. "My outward appearance was very important," she explained in a memoir, "since I had no illusions about my voice." It was no coincidence that her password when traveling with Patton one day was "legs," and on another, "cheesecake." Visiting the 99th Division sector without Bradley, she had to flee when the fighting started with no time to repair her makeup. The inexperienced division would lose three thousand men in four days.

Only slightly less out of touch, Hodges had spent some of his time while the war stagnated hosting morale-boosting baseball heroes Frankie Frisch, Bucky Walters, Dutch Leonard, and Mel Ott, shepherded to the front by St. Louis sportswriter Roy Stockton. That Saturday, before traveling to consult Ike— Bradley, Hodges, and Air Corps major general "Pete" Quesada visited a Belgian maker of custom shotguns who had managed to stay in business profitably during the German occupation. Bradley had already been presented by him with two long-barreled 12-gauge versions, which he hefted proudly to admirers.

Marlene Dietrich also coveted trophy guns. As she visited among the troops, singing throatily what had been the favorite song of the *Afrika Korps*, "Lilli Marlene," she collected confiscated enemy Lugers, all of which were confiscated on her return in 1945 on the orders of the unsympathetic General Marshall— but she managed to conceal and keep a pistol given to her by Patton. Souvenir German guns were also high on GI wish lists.

It was "a sad Christmas," she wrote in a memoir. "Because

of Christmas and because of the lice." (Body lice were unaffected by cold.) "We all felt down, exhausted. It was becoming harder for us to perform with the same enthusiasm as before. . . . Four performances a day, always under enemy fire. Some K rations and coffee, always coffee. Night falls." She learned about delousing powder, which in the back of a tent she had an awed GI apply all over her body. As she traveled with Patton's Third Army she also suffered from severe frostbite, which would affect her fingers and toes the rest of her life. Chilled, she exhausted herself by vomiting away gulps of Calvados, which she drank in excess, although aware of the personal consequences, for temporary warmth. "Patton never demanded that I visit [field] hospitals," she wrote. She did anyway, but refused to tell the wounded "lies. . . . I've too much respect for soldiers to tell them fairy tales, such as 'The war will soon be over' or 'You're not as seriously wounded as it seems.'" Miss Dietrich also charmed her way into Patton's bed, and when Hollywood director Billy Wilder later asked her if her interlude had not indeed been with Eisenhower rather than Patton, she remarked, "But, darling, how could it have been Eisenhower? He wasn't even at the front?"*

Although slowed by icy roads en route to Eisenhower's headquarters on the sixteenth, Bradley detoured via Paris to have lunch at the Ritz with his aide Major Chester Hansen, arriving in Versailles in midafternoon. While Bradley was still in conference at dusk, a message arrived for Eisenhower's British intelligence chief, Major General Kenneth Strong: "This morning the enemy counterattacked at five separate

---

*A more serious, discreet, and long-standing intimacy began then with Major General James Gavin of the 82nd Airborne, who was lean, handsome, and seven years younger than Dietrich.

points across the First Army sector." Like Strong, Bradley had dismissed earlier warnings as exaggerated. "Let them come!" Bradley had offered. They were coming.

Patton's staff had been preparing a push through southern Luxembourg into the industrial Saar. Hodges was readying a thrust toward four dams on the Rur (Roer) River east of Aachen. Although knowing little of activity behind the German lines, Eisenhower guessed from Strong's report that a "local attack" would not be made "at our weakest point." It seemed far more than "local." He suggested that Bradley shift two armored divisions to the contested area.

"Where the hell has this sonofabitch gotten all his strength?" Bradley wondered aloud. Later, a junior analyst at headquarters in Versailles, Noel Annan, would explain that intelligence officers at Supreme Headquarters "were regarded as defeatist if they did not believe the end of the war was in sight."

Now that a broad attack against Hodges's First Army positions was under way, the 10th Armored Division would have to be diverted from Patton's aborted buildup. Bradley warned Eisenhower that Patton wouldn't like it. "Tell him," Eisenhower snapped, "that Ike is running this damned war!" Bradley telephoned and explained why an armored division had to be rerouted toward Bastogne, a crossroads market town of four thousand just west of the Belgian border with Luxembourg. The VII Corps commander there, Troy Middleton, needed help. "God damn it!" said Patton in his unsoldierly high voice. All the Germans wanted to do, he objected, was to derail his offensive. But he conceded the redeployment.

Bradley then called his own headquarters to ask that Lieutenant General William H. Simpson's Ninth Army send down the 7th Armored Division from the panhandle of southern Holland that dipped between Belgium and Germany near Aachen.

Simpson wouldn't like it either, but he would get the division on the move. The Germans appreciated the telephoned exchanges. Most were intercepted.

A corporal in the 7th, Gerald Nelson, in a Sherman tank crew, recalled, "Right before December 16, we were maybe sixty miles north of what became the Bulge [in Verviers, above Spa]. We lived in real buildings, and had cut a Christmas tree from a little cemetery. We found some ornaments and paper to decorate it when word came through to move out. There was mention of a breakthrough but we all thought it was a local one, small. We started out in the afternoon and drove until dark, [and] slept in a column on the side of the road." As they moved south, their destination unrevealed, rumors spread from tank to halftrack that the European war was over. They were being redeployed to the Pacific to bolster MacArthur. Crews in some tanks and trucks quickly scrawled in chalk on the sides of their vehicles, PACIFIC BOUND.

The next morning the division awakened to rain and darkness. To see, Corporal Nelson had to flip down his tank periscope to the position where a rubber blade could sweep the raindrops, which meant that he had to readjust the sights of their 75-mm gun. "About midafternoon as the road through the woods passed a clearing, a shot suddenly missed us. We sped across and then the same thing happened to the tanks behind us." Several officers climbed from their Shermans and conferred, then sent three tanks a mile forward, to an intersection with a few buildings suspected of concealing Germans. Nelson's tank commander, Sergeant Truman Van Tine, told him to turn his .75 just as the turret hatch was hit by small-arms fire, spinning halfway round and stunning Nelson momentarily on his own gunsight. Van Tine jumped out to fire the .50 caliber atop his turret while Nelson poured rounds into the buildings.

A bullet whizzed by his ear and flattened Van Tine to the deck of the Sherman. Nelson pulled him up and applied a first-aid dressing to the hole in his forehead, not realizing that the back of the sergeant's head was gone.

Their sixteen tanks were approaching Poteau, close to the German line on the road which led to St. Vith, the most vital road junction west of the *Schnee Eifel*. They were in the path of the First SS Panzer Division, its advance combat team of 4,000 SS troops, the *Kampfgruppe Peiper*, led by a ruthless twenty-eight-year-old lieutenant colonel, Jochen Peiper. He wanted to reach the Meuse, their primary objective, and had been given his pick of reinforcements. To get an accurate projection of what he could expect from his tanks, he had rehearsed a night drive of fifty miles behind the German lines. Once an aide to Heinrich Himmler, he had also fought in Poland, France, Russia, and Italy, and had a reputation for taking few prisoners. But Peiper did not expect that an outnumbered and raw reconnaissance platoon from the 99th Division's 394th Infantry would be able to delay him for twenty-four hours and blunt his momentum.

A German artillery lieutenant would write in his diary: "The roads are littered with wrecked American vehicles, cars, tanks. Another column of prisoners passes. I count over a thousand men. Nearby there is another column of 1,500, with about 50 officers, including a lieutenant-colonel who had asked to surrender." Taking prisoners to enclosures in rear area locations, rather than interrogating them on the spot for information, was seldom easy in active fighting, as POWs required unavailable manpower to guard them and rations to feed them. The badly wounded and immobile required even more attention. Further, weather and field conditions often made keeping prisoners nearly impossible. Holding POWs in the aftermath of combat, especially those cut off and isolated, was another matter, and their reported numbers then raised unit prestige as they reduced enemy morale. Killing captives was often counterproductive. It made soldiers at risk fight harder if the alternative seemed death by other means.

Bestial SS behavior was another matter, beyond logic. By the second day of the offensive, rumors, most of which were well-founded, spread that SS units were murdering prisoners—soldier and civilian. At least 350 Americans and 100 Belgians were murdered at thirteen locations, 86 alone in the "Malmédy massacre" where soldiers who looked alive after the shooting were dispatched by bullets to the head. A few who feigned death survived and were recovered.

American outrage—and reciprocity—was inevitable. A regiment of the 26th Division issued orders on December 21, which were later publicly if not effectively rescinded: "No SS troops or paratroopers will be taken prisoner, but will be shot on sight." Most of the enemy atrocities were attributed to *Kampfgruppe Peiper* or to the 1st SS Panzers. Octave Merveille, then a boy of thirteen, recalled stories at Huy that the SS had warned that they would kill a Belgian for every American flag found "at the time of liberation." Bitter at SS behavior, American troops killed some captured German troops who wore black, which they identified with the SS. Tank crews, however, were also uniformed in black.

Becoming a prisoner was a chancy matter for both sides. Reportedly an American officer in the 90th Division asked about the disposition of nineteen prisoners sent to the rear, and was told that only five had arrived. On Christmas Eve, General Bradley evinced surprise on learning that four prisoners from the 12th SS Panzers had actually made it to a POW cage. "We needed a few samples," an officer explained.

Brigadier General Bruce Clarke, just awarded his first star and Combat Command B of the 7th Armored Division, had been at Eisenhower's conference in Versailles. He had been en route to a Christmas leave in Paris. Instead, Bradley ordered him and his unit to Bastogne. "Well, there goes Paris," said Clarke. Yet quiet Bastogne at the moment seemed almost a rear area. When a colonel with the 4th Armored Division in Patton's Third Army, he had acquired a reputation for aggressiveness. On a Marshall visit to France, Patton had recommended Clarke for a star, and the chief of staff confessed, "I don't know him." Apparently Marshall then checked him out, as Patton's endorsements were not made lightly. In November, Clarke was promoted and reassigned.

At Vielsalm, a village well north of Bastogne and close to precarious St. Vith, Clarke encountered the hapless General Alan Jones. Thousands of troops, mechanized and infantry, were already on marching orders but few, including the 7th Armored, knew their destinations, which changed depending on reports of enemy advances. Despite inadequate roads, the Germans were moving with vigor. In St. Vith itself, Brigadier General William Hoge's Combat Command B of the 9th Armored Division was bending under the pressure. Much of two regiments of Jones's 106th Infantry, the 422nd and 423rd, were cut off, killed or captured. Their earlier losses in the *Hürtgenwald* had been filled by former ASTP* men, good at textbooks but still green on infantry tactics. Some replacements

---

*Army Specialized Training Program. The armed services assigned some draftees with high intellectual credentials to college programs to educate potential scientists and engineers and (more subtly) to prevent a brain drain into ground units likely to sustain heavy casualties. The academic residencies were known to pleased participants as "All Safe till Peace," but eventually were criticized as elitist and became publicly untenable.

were so new to their outfits that sergeants sometimes didn't get to know their names or hadn't entered them on a company duty roster in the confusion before they had to report them killed or missing.

"Who?" went a repeated query.

"Oh, a couple of new guys."

Bradley had put the largely untried 106th in what seemed the safe Ardennes to gain experience. They did, but too soon. In the 423rd was Lieutenant Alan Jones, Jr., West Point '43. Nearly eight thousand from the division would have to surrender. Distraught and suffering from angina, General Jones was soon felled by a heart attack and evacuated, his military career over.

Vainly brandishing his pistol in St. Vith, General Clarke tried to slow down what GIs readily confessed was "the big bug-out." Legging it out with the rest was a colonel. Clarke was dismayed. A captain in his 23rd Armored Infantry Regiment recalled him as "the highest-ranking traffic cop I have ever seen."

Radioed appeals by both cut-off regiments of the 106th for emergency assistance failed. Ammunition, food, and medical supplies required air drops. The weather was impossible for flights even if the layers of bureaucratic approvals in rear areas succeeded, as they often did not. Their own casualties became grisly replacement sources for those left, who extracted rifles and bazookas, fuel and rations, even boots and helmets, from the dead. The enemy would exploit what they did not. In the village of Honsfeld, from which a surprised regiment of Major General Walter Lauer's 99th Division retreated, the Germans seized fifty workable American vehicles (which did not need ignition keys), some tracked weapons carriers, and jerricans of gasoline to empty into their thirsty panzers. A Mark V Panther gulped 185 gallons per tankful and could not travel far in the difficult Ardennes terrain.

German radio eavesdroppers were already picking up American messages sent urgently in the clear, "We have been bypassed [by the enemy]. What shall we do?"

"Blow up your guns!" was a typical response. Also over-heard dangerously were map coordinates for withdrawal. "Axis Sally," much listened to on GI radios, was soon report-ing American troop movements, mostly backward, in the early confusion. Employing 88s and mortars ahead of them, with tanks following, Field Marshal Model's troops had pushed the *Amis* farther back in two days than they had moved forward in two months. Allied forces had stalled in most places along the Westwall. Much fought over, the border territory had been German at times, Flemish or French at others, and many rivers and towns bore more than one name. Clervaux was also Clerf, the Meuse the Maas, Aachen once Aix-la-Chapelle. All seemed likely to get German tags again.

4

THE REAL THING

In the bloated Sunday papers in the States the gravity of the counteroffensive in the Ardennes remained unrecognized. Censorship and access both had a hand. Buried on page nineteen in *The New York Times* of December 17 was a story under Harold Denny's byline, GERMAN ASSAULTS ON 1ST ARMY FIERCE. Yet the contradictory subhead reassured, "Enemy Pays Heavy Price in Futile Blow to Stem the Advance of Hodges." Hodges had made no advance. Reporting from a First Army rear area nowhere near the action, Denny claimed from the misinformation he was supplied twenty-four hours after the fact that the attacks were "to delay and harass us and make every yard of our advance as costly as possible. . . . These counter-attacks were checked everywhere, usually after hours of severe fighting, and they cost the enemy heavy casualties."

The *Times* front page ignored the Ardennes. Rather, General MacArthur received top billing: AMERICANS CAPTURE AIR-FIELDS ON MINDORO AS SAN JOSE IS WON IN 9-MILE ADVANCE;

SEVENTH ARMY DRIVES DEEPER INTO REICH. Lieutenant General Alexander Patch's 7th Army had captured Wissenbourg, on the prewar French border with Germany north of Strasbourg, and was hardly "deep" into Germany, but readers innocent of maps would have their optimism about a quick end to war enhanced briefly. Large headlines in the *Times* the next day revised the picture downward but balanced the foreboding with further MacArthur successes in the Philippines: NAZI OFFENSIVE PIERCES FIRST ARMY LINES; CHUTISTS AND LUFT-WAFFE SUPPORT PUSH; AMERICANS ADVANCE 6 MILES ON MIN-DORO. On the front page, but still not in the lead story, Harold Denny wrote even more realistically than before: "It now looks like the real thing."

As updates came to General Strong in Versailles, and bulletins were fed to those in the press corps in Paris for Christmas, Eisenhower hurried additional redeployments. Nineteen German divisions had already been identified as in action. The few decent roads through the Ardennes were so crowded with German troops and vehicles that some Nazi generals had to stand in their open staff cars in the snow directing traffic. One dilemma would arise from the *Wehrmacht*'s own strategic ingenuity. To maintain surprise, panzer commanders often exploited narrow pathways, small stream beds, and tracks that were less than roads, all seemingly unusable for armor. If savvy sappers mined them, if a single tank became disabled or ran out of fuel, or if a span unintended to support tons of tracked steel collapsed, traffic was blocked both ways.

In the panhandle Dutch village of Margraten, between Maastricht and occupied Aachen just over the German border, the commandant of the American graves registration company, Captain James Shomon, who managed the improvised military cemetery, heard about the first enemy attacks from the

BBC evening news. He called his lieutenant Ed Donovan, warning that the area could become a paratroop drop zone, and ordering the company on watch. Shomon then called on Burgomaster Herr Ronckers, who had already heard the unhappy news on his own radio.

"Da Boche iss tuff," he said nervously. "Dey can still do much damage. . . . Dis will be a hard Christmas for you Amerikans—and for us." Shomon was thinking of the new graves to come.

By darkness on the first day of the assault, thousands of American stragglers from forward service and support units, and from outfits broken in the first attacks, began clogging roads as they headed rearward, along with refugees from endangered villages. Troops from the 28th Division, already weakened in the *Hürtgenwald* in November, and now smashed near Wiltz, retreated in the cold fog, abandoning many stragglers soon to be prisoners. Major General Norman Cota, the division commander, ordered its unsorted Christmas mail destroyed to keep it out of the hands of the Germans. The few troops who knew what was going up in smoke were those who had watched helplessly as letters, cards, and packages piled up in a courtyard in Wiltz were doused with gasoline and set ablaze.

Scattered in the woods, survivors from the 28th, 99th, and 106th Divisions took days to drift back. Tanks and trucks were sometimes abandoned empty because personnel at fuel dumps had panicked and axed 55-gallon drums of gasoline to keep the contents from Germans nowhere nearby. Still, thousands of gallons were seized from a stalled supply train and from drums erratically parachuted into enemy lines. Newly taken American prisoners were put to work refilling fuel-short panzers from American jerricans.

As his battalions fell apart, Colonel Hurley Fuller of the 110th Infantry Regiment at Clervaux, a veteran of the Argonne in 1918, cranked his field phone to reach General Cota. Fuller wanted permission from Cota, still hazardously at Wiltz, to withdraw to higher ground. It was nearly midnight but Colonel Jesse Gibney, Cota's chief of staff, fudged that the general was at dinner and could not be disturbed. Fuller was to hang tough. "All right, Gibney," Fuller shouted into the telephone. "You're transmitting the general's orders and I've got to obey them. But I'm telling you, it's going to be the Alamo all over again!" Suddenly Gibney heard loud noises on Fuller's end and asked about them. A tank shell had just crashed into his command post, Fuller explained. The town hotel was in the line of fire. He said he was getting out before the Krauts laid the next one in his lap. The phone went silent.

Fuller seized his rifle as smoke filled the room and the hotel corridors. Wounded and dead lay all about. The crimson keystone shoulder insignia of the 28th—the Pennsylvania National Guard division—was known after France in 1918 as "the bloody bucket." Once more it fit the circumstances. A soldier shouted, "Colonel Fuller, I've found a way out of the building. Do you want to take a chance?"

"Hell, yes!" Fuller yelled through the smoke. "Does anyone else want to go?"

Other voices claimed interest, but one added, "I'm blind. I'm blind in both eyes." Fuller had the GI clutch his belt, and, in the darkness, while Clervaux burned, they climbed down an iron ladder laid toward the ground to a slope behind the hotel.

By first light Fuller had lost the blind soldier and several others, and was down to four companions, all plodding west. He would soon be a POW, like many others from the 28th.

Most were draftees. A career officer, Fuller assumed that he was finished even if he survived the war.

Southwest of Wiltz, in early dawn, Master Sergeant Victor Brombert, after a night with other soldiers in a cellar occupied by a family "who added their wails and loud prayers to the screaming of the incoming shells," found "a grim-looking General Cota himself" at the edge of a sloping field. Pistol in hand, he was ordering the remnants of his troops to make a stand, screaming, "I'll shoot any bastard who runs." A German tank materialized out of the fog and snow, "swiveled its obscene muzzle and hit our ammunition truck, lighting up the macabre silhouettes of the trees. General Cota had singled me out, together with a few others, to organize the defense. The huge explosion put an end to our stand. Everyone was on the run again."

Although dazed, Brombert found his jeep, and his team jolted off, looking for an escape route to the north of Bastogne. Through maps, luck, and instinct they made it to the village of Awaille, on the River Amblève, where he encountered his cousin Ossia, a paratrooper with the just-deployed 82nd Airborne. They fell into each other's arms. Both had been refugees to America after France fell. There was little time for conversation, but Ossia would manage to send a letter to his wife in New York about encountering Victor, whose parents assumed he had been taken prisoner. The Germans had filmed the streams of captives being marched eastward, and the propaganda ploy quickly made it through neutrals into American movie newsreels. One sad face under a tilted helmet erroneously suggested Victor. His father somehow obtained a still from the newsreel to assure himself that his son was alive.

To stem the offensive, Eisenhower alerted two airborne

divisions, both then refitting with replacements after Montgomery's Arnhem debacle. Men of the 101st, at Mourmelon-le-Grand, a garrison town near Reims, had been happy to be stationed where Christmas packages could reach them. Paris beckoned; Reims was famous for its bubbly; and a Champagne Bowl football game was planned for Christmas Day, with a turkey dinner to follow. Troops were practicing for the match-up between the 506th and the 502nd Regiments. Then came the radioed alert. That Sunday evening at local cinemas, projectors ceased rolling and lights went on. Officers strode onstage to announce that all passes had been canceled, and that troops would be leaving Reims to resume action. The division was to bolster Troy Middleton's VIII Corps area as light infantry.

The 82nd Airborne had been settling into its billets at Suippes and Soissons to refit. Some troops were already on brief leaves to Paris. Wearing their easily recognizable uniforms, they were quickly seen about, and a staff officer commented to a rear-area colleague, "Those paratroopers are the smartest, most alert-looking soldiers I have seen."

"Hell, man," said the other, realizing that they had been in Montgomery's botched Arnhem operation in Holland in September, "they should be. You're looking at the survivors."

Similar in size to the 82nd, the 101st with replacements had 11,840 men; hundreds were on leave in Paris and expected to bring back supplies for Christmas parties. At Eindhoven during the Arnhem debacle the 101st had lost 3,792 men—killed, wounded, and missing. Major General James Gavin assumed that his outfit would get another major assignment, perhaps to seize bridgeheads over the Rhine in early March. He did not expect, as he was preparing for dinner on the evening of December 17, an urgent telephone call from the former chief of staff of the 82nd, Colonel Ralph Eaton, now moved up to the XVIII (Airborne) Corps headquarters. Ridgway was in England. Taylor, the commanding general of the 101st, was conferring in Washington. Gavin was acting Corps commander; and the situation to the east, he now learned from Eaton, was critical.

Gavin activated movement orders for the 82nd and 101st and arranged for vehicles from motor pools to move both divisions. The general himself was to report to Hodges at what Gavin thought would be Spa. (He did not know that Manteuffel's Fifth Panzer Army headquarters had immediately intercepted the radioed orders.) On December 17, trucks and trailers from the Transportation Corps began hauling 60,000 troops from rear areas, with their ammunition, rations, medical supplies, and spare gasoline, toward the Ardennes. At nine in the morning on the 18th in Mourmelon, the first of 380 trucks began loading battalions of the 101st for the bumpy, unsettling run. By eight in the evening the last men were en route, the convoys motoring with lights on until approaching the Belgian border.

In Wiltshire, the 17th Airborne, in training exercises which Matthew Ridgway was observing as commander of the XVIII Airborne Corps, was posted to France, as were the 11th Armored and the 75th Infantry. Belatedly awakened at 2:15 a.m. on the 18th, Ridgway was given Eisenhower's orders to get going. His 17th Airborne would follow to a reserve position at Givet, on the Meuse in France just short of the Belgian border.

An hour before midnight on Sunday the 17th, Brigadier General Anthony C. McAuliffe, artillery chief of the 101st Airborne and acting commanding general in the absence of Maxwell Taylor, had gathered the division staff and told them, "All I know of the situation is that there has been a breakthrough and we have to get up there." He left Reims early on the 18th, jeeping ahead of his troops to make forward arrangements.

Pausing at Bastogne to get an update, McAuliffe learned that his instructions had been changed. The threatened crossroads town was to be held, and the 101st was to help do it. His troops were rerouted. Instructions from General Gavin were to prepare the area "for all-around defense and to stay there until . . . further orders." As historian Russell Weigley would put it, "In an old American tradition, the 101st would have to form a circle and fend off the Indians until the cavalry reinforcements arrived, in this instance in the form of [old cavalryman] George Patton's Third Army tanks."

Troy Middleton was ordered to remove his VIII Corps headquarters from Bastogne southwest to Neufchâteau, leaving behind the 10th Armored Combat Command, to support the 101st Airborne. His staff regretted abandoning stocks of wine and whiskey which had been carefully stashed away for Christmas and New Year's Eve. The veteran Colonel William L. Roberts of the 10th Armored, who had been in France in 1918, didn't like the orders either. Airborne generals were relative youngsters. He would be outranked.

The youngest paratroop general was James Gavin, acting XVIIIth Airborne Corps commander, who after setting up blocking positions for the 82nd Airborne with Hodges's depleted army near Werbomont, had jeeped south to "issue General McAuliffe his orders in person." He wanted to find out for himself what was happening. Gavin found concern and confusion. "Vehicles were being loaded, and members of the [VIII Corps] staff seemed to be hurrying away. Corps headquarters was in a schoolhouse. I met General Troy Middleton. . . . I also talked to members of his staff. They had no solid information except that the situation was quite fluid and that they were leaving."

Gavin also learned that the 28th Division "had evidently been overrun, and they were uncertain what had happened to it." He soon talked to some of its headquarters officers, "who were quite depressed and disturbed, not knowing the whereabouts of their division." As further troops of the 28th and other shattered units trickled in, they were ordered to the relative safety of Neufchâteau. Most were down to one blanket for every two men. Cut into strips, the blankets had been at least useful for wrapping feet. Boots with liners seemed to footsore GIs never to leave rear areas.

A few kilometers short of Bastogne, the 101st trucks, usually with "colored" drivers as most were restricted, in a segregated army, to service units, offloaded men to march the rest of the way eastward in the snow. It quickly became clear why the trucks had stopped where they did. As columns proceeded on both sides of the road toward Bastogne, clusters of routed troops came stumbling down the middle in disarray, many—despite the freezing weather—without their weapons, packs, even their coats. Some shouted in panic, "Run! Run! They'll murder you! They'll kill you! They got everything, tanks, machine guns, air power, everything!" Including, it would turn out, abandoned American trucks, tanks, artillery, and jeeps.

"They were just babbling," Lieutenant Richard Winters recalled. "It was pathetic. We felt ashamed." But the men of the arriving 101st were also shaken.

Leaving Bastogne just after dark (sunset was at 4:45), Gavin just missed the spearhead of advancing German columns moving west, well behind the retreating rabble. At Werbomont, where he was first headed, the first vehicles of the 82nd were beginning to arrive. In the early darkness, Sergeant Lou Berrena, in charge of a mortar section of the 517th Parachute Infantry, climbed out of his truck into chaos. "The first thing we did," he recalled, "we got fired on by our own machine guns." Anyone unidentifiable was the enemy.

"What the hell is going on?" one of his crew shouted. Berrena then saw a column of American soldiers straggling up the road. "These guys had hardly any equipment. Their guns were gone. And they say it's a mess. And all their tanks are coming back." A straggler told Berrena he was glad the reinforcements had come, and was informed that only a single battalion had made it so far. "A battalion?" said the infantryman. "Hell, there are divisions of Germans out there. I'm not kidding you. You'll never stop them!" No Germans came. Berrena found shelter for the night in a barn.

Holding a quieter 3.000-yard line near Simmerath, on the German border with Belgium below Aachen, the 78th Division, later reinforced with replacements stripped from the 69th Division in England, was offered a bonus. Major General Edwin P. Parker, Jr., promised a Bronze Star Medal and a leave to Paris to any soldier who knocked out a tank with a bazooka. No one would qualify. German tanks clanked elsewhere. American 2.36-inch bazooka fire ("table tennis balls") could not penetrate the front plate of a Tiger tank, a continuing procurement blindness that would cost thousands of casualties, even into the next (Korean) war. To use this weapon successfully, bazooka handlers had to aim at the treads, or the thinner sides, or rear, of an enemy tank. No easy matter.

The assault on St. Vith to the south bypassed the 78th, which was pinned down in the cold fog and snow by artillery barrages. Troops began backtracking, digging in toward Röttgen, to hold more favorable ground. Not all units learned of the orders to withdraw overnight, but their endangered positions would become untenable if St. Vith fell. Uninformed that the 310th Regiment was pulling back, burly Captain Morris "Spearhead" Crane, his name reflecting how far forward his medical detachment remained, was setting up a field hospital. As soon as Crane realized that his men would be all alone across the border, he pulled them back in the darkness and under fire.

Late the next day, Bastogne was the only key road junction in the Bulge still in Allied hands. St. Vith, to the east and untenable, was being evacuated. Trapped, many GIs were taken prisoner. More Germans became available southward to surround Bastogne. Their artillery could reach every point in the town. Locals hid in their cellars and lived on hoarded provisions.

Montgomery repositioned his troops in lower Holland and upper Belgium without engaging them in the fighting. Having downplayed German potential only a few days earlier, he now offered extravagant forecasts that there was little to prevent the *Wehrmacht* from "bounding the Meuse and advancing on Brussels." The British 6th Airborne was ordered from England to bolster his reserves. Perversely pleased that Eisenhower's "broad front" strategy of maintaining pressure everywhere while allegedly dissipating his strength was not working, he felt reassured, despite his mid-September failures, that his idea to concentrate force was the proper formula. He could now survey seemingly certain new opportunities.

Since even generals had to attend to their appetites, and perhaps also as a demonstration of coolness under pressure, Eisenhower, with his headquarters staff and guests in Versailles, enjoyed a dinner of stewed and fried oysters, with champagne. (The oysters were the gift of Stephen Early, White House press secretary, via the New England Seafood Company in Boston.) Averse to shellfish, Bradley asked for scrambled eggs. Afterwards, over five rubbers of bridge with Eisenhower, players drank scotch and bourbon until well after midnight. Unaware that he would soon be supplanted by Montgomery, Bradley left for Luxembourg City in the morning.

Many Americans trapped in the early assaults were herded in long rows to POW cages at Prüm or Gerolstein, beyond the Westwall. One was a nineteen-year-old private in the 28th, William J. Shapiro, who had been knocked unconscious by a shell blast. He awoke in an aid station in Clervaux and watched medics carry in wounded on litters. By evening he could hear machine-gun fire getting closer. He also heard someone say that they were surrounded and had to surrender, and soon another voice warned through the buzz in his head, "If you're a Jewish GI, throw your dog tags away because there are SS troops here."

Shapiro peeled off his two metal dog tags marked with his name and *H* for Hebrew, and threw them into the glowing potbelly stove in the room. The service system was to use a *C* for Catholic or a *P* for Protestant or an alternative initial to indicate the preferred ritual of interment and to identify the grave. (The second tag was retained to register the death.) He had not realized the added risk from the Nazis to which the *H* made him vulnerable.

With hands above his head like the others, Shapiro submitted to a search by the Germans, who took his gold ring. The next morning he was in a column of prisoners trudging eastward into Germany. GIs learned how to sleep standing up. It was easier in clusters of three—that is, for about fifteen minutes, until someone in the human pillar lost balance. After walking for several days—no one was sure of the number—

they reached the railhead at Gerolstein. Dogs barked as the GIs were loaded into boxcars, each man packed in like a can in a carton. Some groaned from wounds. No sanitary facilities existed, and the carriages became increasingly foul. Some died; it was easier than living. Food, if any, consisted of a piece of bread one day, some water the next.

On Christmas Eve, when Allied bombing of the rail lines near the Rhine began, the shock waves seemed to lift the boxcars off the rails, then drop them with a crash. In the lulls between raids, Shapiro and the others heard Germans, despite the clattering of the moving train, singing Christmas carols, very likely from towns they passed through. Similar experiences were recalled by other prisoners being removed from the burgeoning Bulge.

Lieutenant Lyle Bouck of the 394th Infantry Regiment, 99th Division, was stunned in his foxhole by an explosion on the first day of the fighting, pulled out by the Germans and sent plodding in the snow toward Germany. A persuasive major with impeccable English interrogated him. Bouck evaded giving any information but the required name, rank, and serial number, but was pressed further. "Do you see all those tanks out there? Do you have any idea how your army is going to stop this attack? We have jet airplanes that will knock out your air corps. We have secret weapons which will end the war quickly. We'll be in Paris by Christmas. You'll go home, [but] not [as] a winner."

Prisoners were loaded into boxcars, seventy-two counted out for each carriage. Two days later, each POW got a piece of black bread and a tin of hot, bitter ersatz coffee. In six days they had two more hunks of bread, moistening dry tongues with the frost scraped off metal surfaces. Since the temperature was well below freezing, the dead, happily, did not decompose quickly. Prisoners argued and cursed as more of them died. On Christmas Day the train jolted to a stop at Nuremberg, and prisoners received further slabs of bread. Hollow-eyed and trembling, they were now more passive. At a crowded prison camp at Hammelburg, officers and ranks were separated for redisposition.

For Phil Hannon of the 81st Combat Engineers, whose undestroyed vehicles had been seized by the Germans several days before Christmas, the first food available was frozen apples still hanging from trees where the POWs were being held. The fruit hung too high to reach and had to be shaken down. Many GIs were too weak to do that. "This is where your latrine will be," one SS soldier said, pointing to a corner of a courtyard. "If anyone tries to escape, he will be shot." With the holidays close, their thoughts wandered toward home, and they filled the time wanly singing carols. The Germans complained that it kept them awake and threatened to shoot if the songs didn't cease.

The next morning, wet with frost, prisoners were marched to a village occupied by a panzer grenadier regiment, where a few raw potatoes were thrown toward them—nearly a thousand men—and some were stopped to be stripped of their boots. As they scrambled for the potatoes, the Germans laughed.

A Polish guard took some POWs to a house where he distributed boiled potatoes and they filled their canteens with water. Knowing no English, he motioned to them to stuff potatoes in their overcoat pockets. The march continued to Prüm, where more raw potatoes were thrown to them by French forced laborers. Stumbling to a nearby railhead at two in the morning, they were left there in the open until eleven, sleeping fitfully and awakening to be issued rations of hardtack and cheese, one per group of seven. Some riskily drank water from filthy ditches. In the railyards as they waited for trains further eastward, an old man and his wife offered them fresh water, and then worked "like horses hauling water for us until the guards stopped them." The boxcars on which the POWs were loaded still had straw with clinging manure droppings on the floors. Dysentery became common; shouts were heard for "the helmet, for Christ's sake." Foully reeking helmets were passed from hand to hand and emptied out the window. As water on the train grew short, some prisoners became delirious. Guards seemed not to notice.

On December 23, their long train rumbled to a stop in a railyard alongside another line of cars crowded with POWs wearing the keystone patch of the 28th Division. That night, Hannon recalled, an engine chugging by suddenly stopped. The engineer and fireman jumped out and ran. GIs heard the drone of planes overhead. "I watched from the [boxcar] window and saw my Christmas tree. The lead plane dropped a flare. It burst about 200 feet in the air, took the shape of a pine tree. The burning lights were red, purple, orange, and yellow, looking quite like Christmas tree lights."

As bombs fell, prisoners were hustled out of the train toward a frozen ditch. Water had seeped under the surface of the sooty ice. Scooping with their hands, they drank frenziedly. When the bombing faded, they were ordered back into their boxcars. Eight had been killed and thirty-six injured. The next day, Christmas Eve, they were each fed a twelfth of a loaf of bread with some jam. It was more than their stomachs could handle; many were sick. But when night came, from somewhere along the line of boxcars Christmas carols echoed weakly. Back and forth, the carols came—"Deck the Halls," "Silent Night," "O Little Town of Bethlehem." On Christmas Day the train clattered into Frankfurt, and the POWs were marched eastward to Stalag IX-B at Bad Orb. En route some caught a glimpse of a German newspaper poster at a kiosk, which translated as 35,000 AMERICANS CAPTURED. Although an exaggeration, it did not seem to be propaganda.

For Richard McKee of the 106th, whose officers had surrendered his battalion on December 18, there were no boxcars, only an agonizing 137-mile march in the frost to Prüm, the river town west of the winding Rhine. "On the way we met only horse-drawn German guns and soup kitchens headed to the front. On the road we saw many GIs killed a day or so earlier. They were still in their long overcoats and were frozen where they died. Only their shoes were missing." At Gerolstein, prisoners were given cheese and crackers. McKee lost track of time as they spent nights in chicken coops and stationary boxcars and endured strafing by day from Allied aircraft. On Christmas Eve, huddling away from the snow in a farmer's shed, McKee and his POW companions found a barrel of molasses. Somehow their find was spooned out crudely the next day; it became the prisoners' entire Christmas dinner. Many became noisily sick.

In the U.S., newspaper headlines had become larger and more gloomy, although the Pacific still furnished some balance: GERMANS DRIVE 20 MILES INTO BELGIUM; ALLIED FLIERS POUND TANK SPEARHEADS; 742 JAPANESE PLANES SMASHED IN ONE WEEK. The inflated enemy aircraft losses were the good news; the bad was that the Japanese were now employing deadly *kamikazes*—suicide pilots. Their technology was not up to the German V-1 and V-2 robot bombs and rockets.

Far off in Paris—decadent Paris was always a party—the bad news from the Ardennes got out quickly as officers on pre-Christmas leave were alerted, if they could be found in hotels and eateries, bordellos and clubs, to return to their units. In holiday mood, some troops—even lowly GIs—were still arriving. A routine report from the 4th Division command post in Luxembourg at 9:00 a.m. on December 16 noted, with a misspelling, "G-2 left CP for a three-day pass to civilazation." (Apparently few G-2s—intelligence officers—were needed at forward command posts.)

At a posh Parisian restaurant, Lieutenant General "Tooey" Spaatz was hosting a lavish dinner on the seemingly limitless headquarters tab for visiting brass. Seeking attractive women who spoke English for his table, he invited correspondent Mary Welsh, Ernest Hemingway's mistress (later his wife) and then a correspondent for *Time* and *Life*.

The grizzled "Papa," now forty-five but looking twenty years older, had been off to a girlie revue at the Lido with Brigadier General Joseph "Red" O'Hare and Lieutenant Colonel Chester Hansen, both on Bradley's headquarters staff, which was so bloated that the missing were hardly noticed. Red, Mary Welsh learned, "is going back to get some soldiers." She meant back to Washington, to appeal for more riflemen, to keep the War Department from assigning more allotments to the Pacific. "We saw," Hansen recalled, "barebreasted girls do the hootchie-kootchie, until it was late." He would soon be hurrying back to the Bulge.

As the round of courses continued, Mary Welsh noticed that aides with anxious faces kept sidling up to General Spaatz with messages. There was a big story coming, she realized, and after the dessert she offered excuses and told him that she was returning to her hotel, the Ritz. (It was one of the upscale VIP establishments run by an army major on Lieutenant General J.C.H. Lee's staff, Eddie Doerr.) Spaatz offered her his staff car and driver, and—a novelty—an armed airman as escort. Something was indeed up.

The Ritz lobby was chaotic. Officers rushed in and out. Armed soldiers hung about. Whiskey-sodden and hardly up to his war-correspondent credentials, Hemingway pushed through. Upstairs, where he shared a book-littered room with two brass beds, he told his alarmed young brother Leicester, an enlisted man in a documentary film unit, "There's been a complete breakthrough, kid. This thing could cost us the works. Their armor is pouring in. They're taking no prisoners." Then he zonked out, feverish with flu and groggy with drink.

In the morning—it was Sunday the 17th—he recalled through his haze the news of the night before. Paris was always fun—he had even participated drunkenly in its liberation in August. But having been with the troops in Normandy, and in the Ardennes in September, he wanted more action. Pulling strings, he reached Major General Raymond O. "Tubby" Barton of the 4th Division in Luxembourg, in action since D-Day. Hemingway wanted to know, Barton recalled, "if there was a show going on which would be worth coming up for." Otherwise, since he was feeling sick, he would find passage home. For security reasons, Barton said affably, he could offer no details on the wire, "but it was a pretty hot show and to come on up." He did not say that he had just telephoned Bradley, "If you don't get the armor up here quickly, you'd better get set to move [out]."

Red O'Hare, also at the Ritz, had arranged for a jeep and driver, Hemingway told Leicester. Correspondents were forbidden to carry weapons and Hemingway had already been admonished in Normandy, but he instructed his brother, "Load those clips. Wipe every cartridge clean. The Germans have infiltrated guys in GI uniforms." He struggled into two fleece-lined jackets, one over the other, a Kraut souvenir he had procured in the *Hürtgenwald* in November and a leather air-force type familiar in the American press from photos of MacArthur. Before leaving, Hemingway handed Mary a canvas bag of his papers, telling her to burn them if she had to flee Paris. He also gave her an envelope with instructions not to open it before Christmas.

5

RETREATS

As the German salients into the Ardennes deepened, American divisions with untested recruits and
green replacements continued to fall back before German armor
and artillery. Troops that had been preparing to renew the
attack were seldom defensive minded—few had dug foxholes,
strung barbed wire, or emplaced mines. Rumors circulated
about paratroopers landing behind them, and of commandos
disguised in American uniforms. The Germans seemed to have
thought of everything.

The *Kampfgruppe von der Heydte*, scheduled to be dropped
near Eupen, east of Verviers, before dawn on Saturday the
16th to support SS general Sepp Dietrich's Sixth Panzer Army,
had been held back a day. The air transports were in poor
condition, and when Lieutenant Colonel Friedrich-Auguste
von der Heydte complained about their age and maintenance,
Dietrich snapped that he was not responsible for the "deficien-
cies of the *Luftwaffe*." In any case, the veteran Nazi commander assured him, they had nothing to worry about. Behind the

American lines were "only Jewish hoodlums and bank managers."

The flights got off in poor weather early Sunday. Dietrich's forces had made disappointing progress toward the upper Meuse against the stubborn 2nd and 99th Divisions, although in the first days the 99th lost 2,200 men. Unable to link up with the delayed Sixth Panzers, Heydte's troops in 112 obsolescent JU-52 and JU-88 transports were scattered by contrary gusts. Some of his chutists had never been airborne before. Heydte himself injured both arms in landing in the wind. Locating only twenty of his bewildered men at first, he eventually assembled three hundred. Their weapons, rations, and radios were blown away. Without weapons and food, they would wander for three days, finally dispersing to evade capture. On the 22nd, weak with exposure, Heydte, a hero of the 1941 airborne invasion of Crete, and a veteran of Normandy, was taken prisoner.

Skorzeny's crews had jumped off in forty captured American jeeps, and German tanks overpainted with U.S. markings. His crews were to seize bridges across the Meuse toward Antwerp, but none would succeed beyond creating suspicion and confusion en route. Some sent false messages, shot up command posts and cut telephone lines, changed directional road signs, misdirected American traffic, and caused a frenzy of changed passwords drawn from postal rates, shoulder patches, baseball, comic books, and the movies. ("Where do the Dodgers play?" "What is Superman's real name?" "Who is Betty Grable's latest husband?") Victor Brombert's jeep was stopped, and its three occupants asked to identify the "Windy City" (Chicago). "None of us knew, for not one of us was a native [-born] American. We had all been naturalized recently, and one of us had a heavy foreign accent." They did some fast talking—none of it in the idiomatic "American" mastered by Skorzeny's men.

The army security system required throwing one's dog tags to a guard, then reciting the embossed serial number back from memory. Complications could follow. "In my British uniform and [Monty's] 21st Army Group markings," David Niven recalled, "I had some anxious moments at the hands of under-standably trigger-happy GIs. Identification papers meant noth-ing. 'Hands above your head, buddy. All right, so who won the World Series in 1940?'"

"I haven't the faintest idea," confessed Niven, who had been filming in Hollywood since 1934 but knew nothing of baseball. The nearest major-league team was in St. Louis. "But I do know," he added quickly, "that I made a picture with Gin-ger Rogers in 1938."

"OK, beat it, Dave, but watch your step, for Chrissake." Very likely he would not have struck out with the sentry at Vielsalm who asked Major Don Boyer of the 7th Armored, while poking a submachine gun into his belly, "Who's Mickey Mouse's girlfriend?"

Some Germans in what Niven and others christened the Trojan House Brigade scored large successes. "Hello, Joe," said a masquerader identifying himself as SS to his surprised prisoners, "We have captured a lot of your buddies."

One *Kommando* turned even more damaging when a pris-oner of war himself, claiming imaginatively under interroga-tion that their mission was to kidnap Eisenhower. After all, Skorzeny had already engineered abductions for Hitler. When that frightening but phony intelligence got to Versailles, the general became a virtual prisoner of his security detail.

Beetle Smith had passed the misinformation to Eisenhower at their morning staff conference on December 20, by which time the abduction rumor had escalated. Several Germans in American uniforms were allegedly sighted near Epernay, south of Reims, in a civilian vehicle on the main road to Paris. By the time Beetle heard of the plot, sixty mythical Germans were approaching to take Eisenhower hostage. The general had to be persuaded to move from his villa in Saint Germain-en-Laye because it was too remote from headquarters, and a vague look-alike, Lieutenant Colonel Baldwin Smith, was chauffeured about in Eisenhower's overcoat, wearing five stars, to distract the nonexistent kidnappers. From a larger guest house on the grounds of the Trianon Palace Hotel, once occupied by former Vichy puppet Marshal Henri-Philippe Pétain, the authentic Eisenhower was driven by a variety of circuitous routes to his office.

At 8:00 p.m. on the eighteenth, General Fritz Bayerlein of the Panzer Lehr Division was weighing what route to take toward Bastogne from Mageret, on one of the few roads from the northeast which tanks could traverse. He had a local Belgian summoned for information. Two hours earlier, the villager claimed (the general should have been skeptical as it was dark soon after four in the afternoon) fifty American tanks, twenty-five self-propelled guns, and forty or fifty other vehicles had passed through Mageret toward Longevilly. A much smaller force than that, it was Lieutenant Colonel Henry T. Cherry's reconnaissance team from Bastogne. Impressed by the opposition allegedly nearby, Bayerlein settled for placing tanks in blocking positions to intercept enemy traffic, and he hesitated about closing in on Bastogne. The helpful Belgian had bought the town a little more time.

Team Cherry was actually positioned west of Longevilly, on the Belgian side of the border with Luxembourg, and west of the grotto of St. Michael. From Flanders south into Luxembourg, local piety was omnipresent. Crossings were often identified by roadside grottos and their saints' names. Approaching Team Cherry—and the Germans—was a long column of stragglers and vehicles from the 9th Armored Division, hampered by clusters of civilian refugees with wagons and carts. While Cherry's men made contact the next morning with the 26th *Volksgrenadiers* of Panzer Lehr, and, outnumbered, fought back, the 9th Armored's remnants were ambushed on the jammed road. Bayerlein estimated that he took, intact, more than sixty American tanks, trucks, jeeps, and self-propelled artillery. Scores of other vehicles near the shrine were left burning, and dead GIs were sprawled in the snow among the sacred images and stone crucifixes.

The nineteenth was a bad day for Bastogne that worsened well into the night and the next morning. The 101st was still organizing its defenses when German raiding parties, disguised in civilian garb to suggest villagers, surprised and overran the division's service area at Mande-St. Etienne, west of the town. Most soldiers fled into Bastogne, but their stores and ammunition were lost. At a westward crossroads the raiders also captured or killed many of the division's medical staff setting up a clearing hospital. Eight officers and forty-four medics escaped after a fight, abandoning their equipment and supplies. Eleven dead Germans were left behind. They wore appropriated army dog tags and had matching pay books, taken from POWs or corpses. Their clothing was a mixture of civilian dress and American uniforms.

In many ways the 101st was handicapped from the start. Because of the poor weather, no glider surgical team could be flown in as replacements, nor could anything else. Fortunately, Bastogne had ample civilian stocks of food, and fewer civilians to feed as many had already fled. Other units in the town had their own supplies and ammunition to share with the chutists. Also, the Red Cross had abandoned a storage dump of doughnut flour, which led to extending rations with monotonous meals of pancakes.

New medical facilities were improvised. When Corporal Gordon Carson of E Company, 506th Regiment, who had been with the outfit since D-Day, was taken to an aid station with foot and thigh wounds a few days after the German raid, he gazed about and thought he had never seen so many wounded men. Calling a medic, he asked, "Hey! How come you got so many wounded people around here? Aren't we evacuating anybody?"

"Haven't you heard?" said the medic.

"I haven't heard a damn thing."

"They've got us surrounded—the poor bastards."

Besieged Bastogne maintained a level of morale that never wavered. Nor did that of the hardy townspeople who had hunkered down. Although without electricity their radios and few telephones were silent, and they had to depend on hoarded food stocks and water hand-carried hazardously from near-frozen streams as more and more mains were broken. The 101st radio-link vehicle, which arrived just before roads westward were severed, furnished telephone and teletype connections, and armored and artillery units had their own signal equipment. Still, tactical communication inside and beyond their perimeter had to be couched in terms that would puzzle enemy eavesdroppers, and often bewildered their own contacts.

At 4th Division headquarters, Barton told Hemingway that his friend Colonel Bob Chance of the 12th Infantry Regiment was "carrying the ball" for the division but that he was under pressure from the 212th *Volksgrenadiers*, who were armed with *Panzerfausts,* the German rocket-launcher improvement on the bazooka. Barton coaxed Hemingway to see to it that "Bob and his outfit" got a "good publicity play" in whatever he would write, but "Hem" was now too feverish to chase after the troops. Instead, he accepted an invitation from Colonel Charles ("Buck") Lanham of the 22nd Infantry to move into his command post near Rodenburg, northeast of Luxembourg City but safely below the action. A regimental doctor dosed Hemingway with sulfa pills and put him to bed, where he seemed likely to remain over Christmas.

When he discovered that the command post now his hospital was a house once occupied by a priest who had been a German collaborator, new energy flowed into the celebrity correspondent from *Collier's.* He arose, searched for, and found, bottles of sacramental wine he expected would be about somewhere. As he emptied each, he carefully urinated into the bottles, labeling them "Schloss Hemingstein, 1944."* With "the fever and all," and the temperature outside at zero, he explained manically to Lanham that he was improvising chamber pots. But later, fumbling in the darkness, he made the mistake of swigging from a bottle which proved decisively not to be from sacramental stock.

By the time Bradley had returned to Luxembourg City, seventeen German divisions were pushing wedges into the American lines. Keeping in mind that armored columns required roads, Eisenhower's staff, spreading a large map of the Ardennes on the floor, identified two towns to hold where east-west routes toward the Meuse converged—St. Vith (soon lost) and Bastogne. They did not need enemy radio intercepts to realize

---

*He had begun calling himself, jokingly, "Hemingstein" when reporting the Spanish Civil War.

that if the Germans could break through into the Belgian low-lands, they could split the British and American armies, and either retake Antwerp or make its harbor unusable.

Opening out his own map, Bradley showed Patton the deepening German bulge. Since the planned offensive toward the industrial Saar was obviously off, his Third Army, Patton said, could have two divisions moving toward the action the next day if necessary, a third the day after. "What the hell, we'll still be killing Krauts." By the time that Eisenhower called for a meeting in Verdun of his senior commanders for Tuesday the 19th, Patton's planners in Nancy were working on a complex pivoting action toward Bastogne. Before he left, his chief of staff, Major General Hobart Gay, was prepared for a launch signal.

Accompanied by Air Marshal Arthur Tedder, Eisenhower arrived in Verdun at eleven in an armor-plated Cadillac he had used since Algiers. Taking no chances that Skorzeny's fake Americans were about, he was escorted by a security detail. The meeting site was closely guarded. Although in one success a *Greif* trooper posing as an MP misdirected an entire battal-ion of the 84th ("Railsplitter") Division, the Skorzeny squads would disintegrate once the offensive began unraveling. Its chief and unintended success was nearly immobilizing the Supreme Commander, who in the furtive days before Christ-mas had never seemed less supreme.

Eisenhower's strategy session was a rare emergence from restraints. A second-floor room of an old French stone bar-racks, surrounded by a sea of mud, was warmed inadequately by a lone potbelly stove, and set up with large easels to dis-play maps. There, Tedder, Bradley, Patton, Devers, and Mont-gomery's deputy Freddie de Guingand and their aides met with the harried Supreme Commander to work out joint moves.

(Monty would seldom deign to travel to lesser generals.) As Eisenhower's own aides, Ken Strong and "Pinky" Bull, arrived a few minutes late, delayed by the bad roads, Ike's impatience clouded over his usually genial facade. "Well," he scowled, "I knew my staff would get here; it was only a question of when."

Unpersuasively, he described the fumbled crisis as an opportunity rather than a "disaster," appealing for "only cheerful faces at this conference table." Farther to the east, as the conferees knew, their surprised divisions were still being mauled. Yet, thinking big as usual, Patton offered, "Hell, let's have the guts to let the sons of bitches go all the way to Paris. Then we'll really cut 'em up and chew 'em up." Some laughed, but Eisenhower cut Patton off sharply with "George, that's fine. But the enemy must never be allowed to cross the Meuse."

Eisenhower wanted the penetration blunted and narrowed. Containing the bulge between Bastogne and St. Vith would limit the few viable roads by which the Germans could move reinforcements and supplies toward the Meuse. Juggling army boundaries, he wanted Jacob Devers's Seventh Army to move up from the south into areas from which Patton had hoped to jump off into the Saar, and Patton to attack the southern flank of the bulge below Bastogne.

Inevitably, as the German penetration divided his zone, Bradley would diminish into a minor player. Since he insisted upon keeping his headquarters in Luxembourg City, staying in touch with Eisenhower by telephone, Bradley's northernmost forces would be closer to Montgomery's command than to his own.

"George," Eisenhower ordered Patton, with a diplomatic nod toward Bradley, to keep him in the picture, "I want you to command this move—under Brad's supervision, of course—making a strong counterattack with at least six divisions. When can you start?"

"As soon as you're through with me," Patton said. "I can attack the day after tomorrow morning." He did not mention that he had left three alternative plans with Hobart Gay in Nancy, anticipating the next move. All he had to do was telephone a code word to activate his troops. But he conceded that of his six divisions Eisenhower had asked for, there were realistically only three. Patton noted in his diary that it "didn't enter his [Ike's] head" that the other divisions called for "exist[ed] only on paper." They had been battered in the *Hürtgenwald* in November and were unready. He had only the reliable 4th Armored, 26th and 80th.

His aide, Lieutenant Colonel Charles R. Codman, recalled "a stir, a shuffling of feet, as those present straightened up in their chairs. In some faces skepticism [showed]. But through the room a current of excitement leaped." Taking tens of thousands of men facing eastward, swiveling them north, and moving them, with their armor and supplies set up for a different thrust, to counterattack over inadequate and icy roads two days later, seemed logistically problematic. Patton was confident he could do it.

Turning toward Bradley as he described his plans for the southern shoulder of the Bulge, Patton contended, "Brad, the Kraut's stuck his head in a meatgrinder. And"—he swiveled his fist in simulation—"this time I have hold of the handle." Replying to questions from others at Ike's table, he deplored their caution. He would have liked to lure the Germans forty or fifty miles too far, then chop them off.

"Don't be fatuous, George," Eisenhower warned, reining in tartly what he assumed was Patton's brag. "If you try to go that early, you won't have all three divisions ready, and you'll go piecemeal. You will start on the twenty-second, and I want your initial blow to be a strong one! I'd even settle for the twenty-third if it takes that long to get three full divisions."

In two hours, the redispositions were settled. As the meeting broke up, Eisenhower walked to the door with Patton. "Funny thing, George," he joked, referring to his new superrank, "every time I get another star, I get attacked." His fourth had come just before the Kasserine Pass embarrassment in Tunisia early in 1943.

"And every time you get attacked, Ike," Patton retorted, "I have to bail you out." Bailing out the Bulge would be one of Patton's finest hours, justifying his belated fourth star, granted when the war was nearly over. Yet Bradley, who had vaulted over the unpredictable Patton, and Eisenhower, who had held him back, both continued to have mixed feelings about entrusting crucial operations to Patton, while continuing to show confidence in Hodges. "I trust," Ike would grumble to Marshall as late as March 12, 1945, "that the Secretary of War will wait for my recommendation before putting Patton's name for promotion. There is no one better acquainted than I with Patton's good qualities and likewise with his limitations. In the past I have demonstrated my high opinion of him when it was not easy to do so. In certain situations both Bradley and I would select Patton to command above any general we have, but in other situations we would prefer Hodges." Grant might not have made the cut in Eisenhower's army.

Later, bespectacled *General der Panzertruppen* Erich Brandenberger recalled in defeat that he expected then "a speedy reaction from the enemy." He meant Patton. The few good roads leading north through Arlon, just west of the Luxembourg border, would be used, Brandenberger guessed, to move Patton's divisions toward Bastogne, but "not earlier than the fourth day of the attack. The fact that these forces would probably be commanded by General Patton made it quite likely that the enemy would direct a heavy punch against the deep [southern] flank of the German forces scheduled to be in the vicinity of Bastogne." In striking southeast out of Normandy the previous summer, Brandenberger acknowledged in ironic self-congratulation, "Patton had given proof of his extraordinary skill in armored warfare, which he conducted according to the fundamental German conception."

From radio intercepts, Brandenberger already knew that the 101st Airborne was reinforcing Bastogne from the west. He expected his Seventh Army to face Patton's armor from the south. Patton moved a day later than anticipated, but unexpected resistance from what remained of mauled and broken American divisions had slowed the German advance from the beginning. Hitler hoped to have troops at the Meuse by the third day of the offensive, but they were struggling at St. Vith and Bastogne, which narrowed their penetration. Von Rundstedt was already appealing in vain to Hitler to curtail the operation as too ambitious for their resources, and characterized the state of the narrow, snowbound roads as "insufficient . . . for the deployment of the army." Stubbornly, Hitler wanted to exploit the December weather, but fuel shortages and the short winter days and early darkness handicapped movement.

On his own as 21st Army Group commander, Monty telephoned Lieutenant General Miles Dempsey of the British Second Army to redeploy their divisions to back up fifty miles of the west bank of the Meuse, and to have tank patrols fan out to patrol all bridge crossings. Showily, Montgomery was inhibiting, without firing a shot, a future German northern thrust that would never come. That done, at 4:15 a.m. on the 20th, awakening early, Monty telephoned his chief of staff in London to insist that someone—obviously himself—take complete charge in the north. The officer at the night desk explained that it was "no good" waking up Brooke, as London had no authority to order Eisenhower about and would have to consult Washington, where it was nearly midnight on the 19th, an impossible time.

Some German troops positioned to follow up the first advances remained mired in traffic jams which tailed back to the Westwall. At the villages of Krinkelt and Rocherath, just inside Belgium in the south, the 12th SS Panzer *Hitlerjugend* armored divisions emerging from the Arenberg Forest also lacked sufficient infantry support, which cost them vehicles. Facing Gerow's V Corps and bogged down, they resorted, as did the Americans, to using immobilized tanks as stationary pillboxes. "I spotted our battalion commander," Lieutenant Willi Engel, in a Panther tank platoon, wrote. "His face registered frustration and resignation. The failed attack and painful losses obviously depressed him severely. The knocked-out Panzers offered a distressing picture. At that moment, a single Panzer approached the Command Post. Suddenly, only about 100 m[eters] away, it turned into a flaming torch. . . . An immobile but otherwise serviceable Sherman had scored the hit. . . . Both sides fought with bitter determination."

Another tank platoon commander, Lieutenant Willi Fischer, recalled, "When I reached the vicinity of the [Rocherath] church, a gruesome picture was waiting. Beuthasser was bailed out [of the hatch]. . . . His loader was killed by rifle fire as he bailed out. . . . Brodel's tank stood next to me, burning brightly. He sat lifeless in the turret. In front of me, more Panzers had been put out of action and were still burning." But the Germans weren't about to withdraw. A grenadier in the 12th SS Panzers painted in block letters on a Belgian farmhouse wall, FÜHRER BEFIEHL, WIR FOLGEN DIR! ("Führer commands; we will follow!")

Reports reaching Versailles remained belated and confused. With time, there was less cut-and-run. Under fire, the 38th Cavalry Reconnaissance Squadron—tankers and supporting troops—on the northern shoulder of the Bulge at Monschau, above Rocherath, laid eighty truckloads of barbed wire, laced with trip-flares and booby traps, then prepared foxholes. Where the ground was too frozen to dig, they employed dynamite. The flank held. The Germans never broke through. The 38th lost fifteen men. Lieutenant Colonel Robert E. O'Brien, Jr., explained it as not "any heroic action, but . . . what an efficient, active defense can do."

Below Monschau in the Forest of Höfen, many in the 99th Division were either casualties or prisoners—or both—but by December 20, Pfc Charles Swann of the 395th Regiment managed to slip past the Germans. Reporting to the L Company commanding officer, he asked about his 2nd Platoon. "You're it," said the CO. Still, Liège and Antwerp, the twin goals of the offensive in the north, could only be reached by erratic V-1 flying bombs, their launching racks positioned well behind the German lines.

As a Belgian barmaid inured to patched windows served cognac to *Life* correspondent Jack Belden in a threatened town liberated three months earlier, another villager confided, "We can stand the buzz bombs. That is nothing. But the Germans. We couldn't stand the Germans here again." In the darkness near Stavelot, guarding the big northern fuel dump, Lieutenant Joseph Couri of the 743rd Tank Battalion watched, from his open turret, the tail glow of pilotless bombs heading toward Liège but could not hear them over the roar of his Sherman's engine. It was not much warmer with the turret closed, as the tank's air intake sucked the frost inside, forming icicles.

In Washington on the twentieth, Secretary of War Henry Stimson noted in his diary, "By this morning they [the Germans] had made quite a good deal of progress. So I had a talk with Marshall over that. We agreed [from reports received] that the Germans could not get very far. . . . Our people do not seem to be rattled and the American forces are closing around the German salient and I think will stop it." What he didn't know was how many units, pressed by superior firepower, had retreated under what General Gavin described as "the classic tactical order": "Let's get the hell out of here."

Hodges, who had abandoned his First Army CP at Spa in apparent panic, had not been invited—or ordered—to the Verdun conference. He had been inexplicably unavailable for two days thereafter, and his chief of staff, Major General William B. Kean, was in de facto command. Later, Kean claimed loyally that Hodges had been "confined to his bed, barely conscious with viral pneumonia," a description suggesting more than a two-day affair, and denied by an observer who saw Hodges despondently "sitting with his arms folded on his desk, his head in his arms."

With the Germans between them, Bradley communicated with Kean by crackling field telephone. "First Army had a very bad staff," the impolitic Beetle Smith later conceded, and "Hodges [was] the weakest commander we had." On his own initiative, "Gee" Gerow used his V Corps to bolster the northern shoulder of the Bulge, and Montgomery, whose Christmas holiday was now aborted, urged Jock Whiteley at Versailles (presumably sympathetic, as he was a Brit) to suggest to Smith that Bradley's depleted armies be put temporarily under Monty's 21st Army Group. Without waiting for Pentagon clearance, Ike would agree. The Bulge had split Bradley's 12th Army Group headquarters in Luxembourg City from the north. He later claimed that the loss of two-thirds of his command to Montgomery was Eisenhower's doing, and that he was "completely dumbfounded—and shocked" by it.

Instead of Ike's "standing up to Beetle Smith," Bradley would write later, reinventing the realities, "and telling him that SHAEF [headquarters] was losing its head, that I had things under control, and reassuring him that Hodges was performing magnificently under the circumstances," Bradley had to "knuckle under" to the facts. He did not concede easily. It was a matter of personal and national pride. Eisenhower's deputy, Ken Strong, could overhear, in Versailles, Bradley shouting over the telephone, "By God, Ike, I cannot be responsible to the American people if you do this. I resign."

"Well, Brad," Eisenhower answered flatly, "those are my orders." Bradley knew he had lost control in the First Army sector as well as in Simpson's Ninth Army area, and he seemed to have been protecting Hodges as well as his own reputation. He worried as well that once the tenacious Montgomery took over a command, he would not give it back.

On the evening of December 20, as the noose of General

Heinrich von Lüttwitz's XLVII *Panzerkorps* began tightening around Bastogne, General Middleton telephoned Colonel Roberts from Neufchâteau about unifying the command structure in Bastogne. Tony McAuliffe would have "the say" in the town. He wore a star. Nevertheless, his "say" might be a short one. Middleton hoped they could hold out until Christmas.

6

MADHOUSE

WITH PATTON'S TURNABOUT IMMINENT, SUPREME Headquarters in Versailles radiated a confidence belied by the circumstances. German resources inevitably would thin out. Eisenhower would protect Bradley during his Christmas season reduction in authority, maintaining appearances. Montgomery issued orders for the northern shoulder of the Bulge, moving Bradley's troops about but committing no British forces to the line. Although Bradley in Luxembourg City was remote from the action, his aide, Chester Hansen, wrote, "[12th Army Group] Headquarters continues to be a madhouse, with too many people running in and out—[and] too many telephone calls. Traffic is heavy, too, with the new divisions coming to reinforce our effort. . . . They have helped at least to abate the alarmist sentiment that was so evident yesterday."

Embarrassed by the loss of much of his command, Bradley was keeping his hand in. He was also anxious about the Skorzeny scare that had nearly immobilized Eisenhower. Believing that he, too, might be targeted kept up Bradley's illusion of significance. "We have removed the [three-star license] plates from the General's jeep," Hansen wrote. "He rides in nothing else, no more sedans."

Alarmist rumors in reverse halted Brigadier General Clarke on the morning of the 20th. Just above St. Vith he was "captured" by American MPs. "I'm General Bruce Clarke," he insisted. He had just abandoned his appropriated Mercedes-Benz, a prize passed on to him by Major General Robert W. Hasbrouck as the 424th Regiment withdrew from St. Vith. What more circumstantial evidence did a GI need than a purported American in a Merc?

"Like hell," retorted an MP. "You're one of Skorzeny's men. We were told to watch out for a Kraut posing as a one-star general." Besides, only a German, on interrogation, would have insisted that the Chicago Cubs were in the American League. But Clarke was no baseball fan. "There's a brand-new star on that car," he appealed to his driver. "Get it please." Although he escaped further embarrassment, he didn't want his first star to become a Kraut souvenir.

Another senior officer, exasperated at a checkpoint by the persistent questions, finally bellowed, "How do I know *you're* not a German soldier?"

"Sir," said the sentry patiently, "don't you know Hitler ain't got no niggers in his army?"*

Even the armored staff car of General Bradley (before he switched to less conspicuous jeeps) was insufficient to exempt

---

*General J.C.H. Lee had many "colored" troops with infantry training, most in supply jobs which took some to the front. A few stayed. When he offered to send "a limited number" to join "veteran units" as replacements, breaking down historic segregation, Eisenhower and Bedell Smith rejected the proposal as contrary to War Department policy. Grudgingly, SHAEF soon accepted only those who volunteered to take a reduction in rank to private. In a month 4,562 did.

him from security checks. He passed the first two password questions, although the MP himself did not know, as Bradley did, that Springfield—not Chicago—was the capital of Illinois. While the general failed on the name of Betty Grable's newest husband, two out of three correct answers sufficed. He did not attempt to visit Hodges, but he did telephone several times—or more—a day, for information.

Monty, rather, employed his wireless intelligence system "Phantom" to liaise with other commands—junior officers who carried information back and forth from headquarters to headquarters in their heads. One LO had already found Hodges in flight from Spa—in bed at 2:30 a.m. in the unpalatial Palace Hotel in Liège. Now Monty in an unusual move checked in personally with Hodges immediately on assuming control of First Army. Accompanied by motorcycle outriders and in an armored car flying British pennants, the field marshal, with his aide Major Carol Mather, turned up flamboyantly at the relocated Hodges command post at 1:30 p.m. on the 20th. On invitation, akin to orders, Simpson joined them. A V-1 had impacted not far off; many of the building's windows were shattered. Monty's stagy arrival, an aide to Hodges recalled resentfully (and as Bradley would repeat to others), was much like "Christ come to cleanse the temple."

Declining lunch, Montgomery also dismissed Hodges's own operations map. Instead of inviting the generals to brief him on their views of the situation in the area, he spread out his headquarters maps on the warm "bonnet" of his Humber staff car, and turning from them to Mather, many degrees lower in rank than the two American generals, barked, "What's the form?" Even the term was graceless, as it was a Britishism for what was happening, or required, very likely unknown to Hodges or to Simpson. "Our American friends,"

Mather recalled, "looked severely discomfited. It was a slight uncalled for."

One personal visit to Hodges seemed enough. Montgomery would turn over Hodges and Kean to "Phantom." On returning, he suggested to Versailles with unusual tact (for him) that although Hodges should be replaced, Eisenhower might want to give him the benefit of some overnight thought. The next day, Freddie de Guingand telephoned Beetle Smith and quoted Monty as advising, in faint praise, after some overnight thought of his own, "Hodges is not the man I would pick, but he is much better [at the moment]."

Using language which echoed months of sour objections about Eisenhower from Field Marshal Brooke, Montgomery telegraphed to London, "There is a definite lack of grip and control; no one seems to have a clear picture as to the situation. . . . I think I see daylight now on the northern front, and we have tidied up the mess and got two American armies properly organised. But I see rocks ahead and no grounds for the optimism Ike seems to feel. Rundstedt is fighting a good battle."

The next day, as Patton began wheeling his troops about, Montgomery telegraphed Brooke again, in gleeful anticipation, "I do not think Third US Army will be strong enough to do what is needed. If my forecast proves true, then I shall have to deal unaided with both Fifth and Sixth Panzer Armies. I think I can manage them, but it will be a bit of a party." Blurring nationalities somewhat, he placed the British 51st Division under Simpson, whom he trusted, and had Simpson's Ninth Army supplemented by two of Lightning Joe Collins's divisions from VII Corps. These would take over part of Hodges's depleted front. (Hodges was largely reduced to an observer.) The remaining British forces would be in reserve, out of the battle.

To Eisenhower, who had suggested shortening the First Army front, Montgomery replied condescendingly, "I have every hope that we shall be able to restore the situation and I see no need at present to give up any of the ground that has been gained in the last few weeks by such hard fighting." But he did. Though he conceded that Hasbrouck's 7th Armored Division had been especially tough around St. Vith, on the twenty-second he ordered the weary division to withdraw, having delayed Manteuffel's 5th Panzers as much as made sense. Hasbrouck appreciated the realignment. Giving up the ground rescued his men.

Eisenhower rationalized to Montgomery that the questionable Hodges was "the quiet reticent type and doesn't appear as aggressive as he really is. Unless he becomes exhausted he will always wage a good fight." Then Ike radiogrammed both Simpson and Hodges, separately, in diplomatic pats on the back, "In the recent battling you and your army have performed in your usual magnificent style." As if they were children, he added, "Now that you have been placed under the Field Marshal's operational command, I know that you will respond cheerfully and efficiently to every instruction he gives."

Although Bradley had worried about Montgomery's tendency to "tweak our Yankee noses," the tweaking first came from Eisenhower. Patton noted scornfully in his diary that the rearrangement in command was "either a case of having lost confidence in Bradley, or having been forced to put Montgomery in through the machinations of the Prime Minister or with the hope that if he gives Monty operational control, he will get some of the British divisions in[to action]. Eisenhower is unwilling or unable to command Montgomery." Realizing that he was now pretty much his own boss, Patton wrote to his wife, Beatrice, that "the staff of the Third Army, which consisted of myself and Sergeant [John L.] Mims [his jeep driver] visited two corps and five division commanders, and telephoned for the engineers, tank destroyers, extra tank battalions, etc."

London papers were full of gloomy reports about how the war was stagnating, or worse, under Eisenhower. Inserting Monty under a figurehead Supreme Commander seemed a last-ditch hope to wrest control of the war—and the peace—for Britain. As Churchill had written to Jan Smuts, and as the press knew, "Our armies are only about one-half the size of the American and will soon be little more than one-third. . . . It is not as easy as it used to be for me to get things done." In that respect, the Bulge was a Christmas gift to Churchill—if he could exploit it. But that required making the British presence appear meaningful. Columns of troops trumped columns of print.

A melodramatic *Daily Express* headline asked, MONTHS ADDED TO WAR? Its story exploited a German radio claim that Liège had been reached—which would never happen—and that fighting was under way "in the city's suburbs." Putting the war into more realistic perspective for the ordinary home-front Englishman, the *Daily Mail* charged, "There is not enough beer in some parts of the country to last over the holidays. Many public houses may have to shut down on Christmas Day and part of Boxing Day."* The Paris correspondent of the *Daily Telegram* dispatched a unique fantasy offshoot of the Skorzeny rumor—that English-speaking German women,

---

*Boxing Day, December 26, originally set aside to give "Christmas boxes" (usually a coin) to servants. The Germans also observed a *Zweite Weihnachtstag*.

carrying knives, had been dropped by parachute into American lines. Reportedly seven had been captured, and confessed that their mission had been to seduce American soldiers, plant knives in their backs, and go on to lure further GIs.

But for headquarters handouts, newsmen enjoying the Christmas season in Paris knew little of the real war. Near Marche, northwest of Bastogne, units of the 84th Division fought off black-uniformed SS troops, accompanied by tanks armed with menacing 88s. Slipping in with grenades and bazookas to attack the rear engines of the heavyweight Tigers through their vulnerable grillwork was hazardous, but disabled tanks cost the Germans armored cover and clogged the few viable roads. The SS had to bypass Marche, and in the renewed quiet, business as usual resumed quickly. Belgian Christmas shoppers emerged warily onto the snowy streets, and Private First Class Roscoe Blunt, nineteen, slipped away from his anti-tank unit to swap prized American cigarettes for a loaf of hot bread and a bottle of wine. While he and his buddies rested, a company officer came by with news that via headquarters radio they could, for ten dollars, wire flowers home for Christmas. Rockie Blunt took up the offer. Months later, he discovered that the telegraphed flowers had been misconstrued by his mother as notification of his death.

As Montgomery was reorganizing at Bradley's expense what Alan Brooke called the Northern Wing, the British Cabinet, from Churchill's accounts, took pleasure in the reversal of command. Still, Brooke remained skeptical of any management of troops whatever left to allegedly unskilled American generals who had "mishandled" the war. "If only the Americans are up to it," he wrote scornfully in his diary. "Ike," he concluded, "is a hopeless commander." Then he added further skepticism. "German offensive appears to be held in the north, but I am a little more doubtful about the south. Patton is reported to have put in a counterattack. This could only have been a half-baked affair and I doubt it's doing much good." Despite his private bluster, Brooke cabled Montgomery not to gloat over his new authority.

"This is the year's shortest day," Eisenhower wrote grumpily to Mamie from his imposed confinement on the evening of the 21st, "how I pray that it may, by some miracle, mark the beginning of improving weather!" Then he added, darkly, "There are so many things about this war that cannot be told now—possibly never—but they should make interesting talk between you and me when we're sitting in the sun, taking our elegant ease in our reclining days."

From Luxembourg, working the telephones via his command post in Nancy, Patton confidently ordered his units about the map, hoping for better weather and worsening German fuel problems. Captured tank crews reported stranding armor for lack of gas, and intercepted radio messages revealed enemy desperation to seize fuel stores. "I wish it were this time tomorrow night," he told his diary. "When one attacks, it is the enemy who has to worry. Give us the victory, Lord."

Getting updated, Stimson sat in on a staff meeting at the Pentagon with Marshall, writing afterwards in his diary, "The news from France was bad again today, although our troops seem to be slowing up the breakthrough somewhat. Still, it is a very formidable threat. . . . It may lengthen the war." Some soldiers had fled, and many others, cut off, had surrendered, but a redeeming aspect of the crisis, which Marshall and Stimson recognized, was that even broken American divisions, evidencing courage and resourcefulness, had slowed, if not blunted, the German offensive beyond expectations on both sides. The Bulge was producing little strategic benefit. Lengthening the war only increased the casualties.

Washington continued to worry about what was *not* happening in the East. In a winter freeze, the Russian front was relatively quiet, and both Marshall and Eisenhower realized that Hitler might risk more temporary withdrawals of forces and materiel to the Bulge. To Marshall on December 21, Eisenhower cabled, in an ambiguous cover-up, "Bradley has kept his head magnificently and has proceeded methodically and energetically to meet the situation. In no quarter is there any tendency to place any blame on Bradley. I retain all my former confidence in him." Yet Bradley had little control of events. Less confidently at home, Stimson held his weekly press conference, assuring newspapermen who saw a dark Christmas ahead, "We will have them." He reminded them about his own experience as an artillery colonel in 1918, when the Germans opened a win-the-war offensive that flamed out far short of reversing defeat.

On Friday morning the 22nd Hemingway felt up to seeing how the Bulge was being fought. Colonel Jim Luckett of the 4th Infantry's 12th Regiment and Colonel Buck Lanham of the 22nd Regiment, now a good friend, invited "Hem" to drive with them to watch the war from a hilltop about two miles from the village of Michelshof. In the *Hürtgenwald* on November 22, four weeks earlier, during an attack on Lanham's command post, Hemingway, again flouting orders regarding newsmen and weapons, had seized a Thompson submachine gun and fired away, killing several Germans and probably saving Lanham's life.

From a snowy hillside, the three war tourists observed the action. Two battalions of Major General Leroy Irwin's 5th Infantry in Patton's Third Army were to attack, over rugged terrain, in the direction of Echternach on the River Sauer. The river there was the border with Germany, well to the north of unendangered Luxembourg City. Cold fog began to drift in just as the 5th Infantry's shelling began. Footsoldiers in white snow-camouflage "spook suits," fashioned from Belgian bed sheets, followed, became lost in the gloom, and were quickly under enemy artillery fire. Taking unexpected punishment, they withdrew. Neither the two colonels nor Hemingway could see anything.

Lanham and Luckett joked about the episode but confusion under fire wasn't funny, nor were the casualties. The trio jeeped back to "Tubby" Barton's command post in Junglinster, halfway to Luxembourg City. Barton was about to return to the States, officially because of ill health. (His senior staff assumed that Eisenhower had relieved him because he had bungled in the Hürtgen the month before, taking five thousand casualties.) A farewell Christmas Eve party was being planned, and their talk was of food and drink to come. Marshall would offer Barton a Stateside training command.

Before leaving Junglinster, Hemingway, gray-bearded and massive in his two fleece-lined coats, one over the other, and flanked by the mustached, sturdy Barton and the equally mustached Chance, posed for a photo. Through Mary Welsh, what Hemingway thought he saw near Echternach and reported was rewritten in the *Life* offices. Patton knew little about the unsuccessful affair. It was a diversion, a sideshow. He was intent on driving toward Bastogne.

* * *

In the face of the facts, Eisenhower cabled the War Department to recommend both Spaatz and Bradley for four-star rank. It would have "a fine effect," he argued, seen as evidence of "calm determination and courage in the face of trials and difficulties." Having no idea yet how little involved Bradley was, or how overshadowed Spaatz was by Eisenhower's British air advisers like Tedder, Marshall replied only that Congress was recessed for the Christmas holidays and that no action would be feasible. Eisenhower conceded on December 23 that he understood. He had forgotten about Christmas in Washington.

On the twenty-third Eisenhower also issued an Order of the Day, meant more for newspapers at home than for men in the field who had no opportunity to read it. His first since D-Day, it urged turning Hitler's "great gamble into his worst defeat" and called upon troops "to rise now to new heights of courage, of resolution, and of effort. Let everyone hold before him a single thought—to destroy the enemy on the ground, in the air, everywhere—destroy him!" He closed with a reflex reference to "God's help," but with no mention of the imminence of Christmas. Nevertheless, hidden German loudspeakers began blaring toward the American lines, as troops of the 310th Infantry Regiment (78th Division) heard: "General Eisenhower acknowledges that the great German offensive which started on December 16 is a greater one than his own. . . . How would you like to die for Christmas?"

Eisenhower also dictated a long self-protective memorandum for his file to his public relations aide, Captain Harry Butcher, summing up the first week in the Ardennes for a report to Marshall. Ike had just received Christmas greetings from the general expressing cautious appreciation for a "magnificent job" and skirting recent events. "Largely through your leadership, in force, in wisdom, and in patience and tolerance, you have made possible Allied cooperation and teamwork in the greatest military operation in the history of the world, complicated by social, economic and political problems almost without precedent. Good luck to you in the New Year. May the Lord watch over you. You have my complete confidence."

With obvious relief, Eisenhower replied that Marshall's Christmas letter was "the brightest spot in my existence since we reached the Siegfried Line.* Short of a major defeat inflicted on the enemy, I could not have had a better personal present."

The Christmas gift that Patton desperately wanted was clearing weather, to better move his armor and for air support of his operations. On returning from Verdun, as his divisions were about to turn north, he told his Third Army senior chaplain, Colonel James O'Neill, that he was going to use a prayer he had O'Neill compose earlier when rain was delaying the abortive attack into the Saar. "Do you have a good prayer for weather?" he had asked. "I'm tired of these soldiers having to fight mud and flood as well as Germans. See if we can't get God to work on our side."

"May I say, General," the chaplain ventured, "that it isn't a customary thing among men of my profession to pray for clear weather to kill fellow men."

"Are you teaching me theology or are you the Chaplain of the Third Army? I want a prayer." Well read, including all of the Bible, Patton knew that there were many pre-battle appeals to the Almighty in Scripture.

Since Father O'Neill realized that Patton did everything over the top, he duly wrote something for the general, beginning, "Almighty and most merciful Father, we humbly beseech

---

*The *Westwall* fortifications, based upon the prewar Siegfried Line.

Thee, of Thy great goodness, to restrain these immoderate rains with which we have to contend. Grant us fair weather for Battle. Graciously hearken to us as soldiers who call upon Thee that armed with Thy power we may advance from victory to victory and crush the oppression and wickedness of our enemies, and establish Thy justice among men and nations. Amen."

The rains of early December had now congealed into snow, and the Saar offensive for which the supplication had been intended had been canceled. When O'Neill reminded him of that, Patton said, "Oh, the Lord won't mind. He knows we're too busy now to print another prayer." Patton had it set in type in Luxembourg City and distributed in wallet size, with a holiday greeting on the other side that wished "each officer and soldier," incongruously in the circumstances, "a Merry Christmas." More to the point, he added, "I have confidence in your courage, devotion to duty, and skill in battle. We march in our might to complete victory. May God's blessing rest upon each of you on this Christmas Day."

Patton was not invoking the Almighty to fulfill wartime expectations for elevated faith, as in Eisenhower's D-Day message about a "Great Crusade," or Roosevelt's nationwide radio prayer that evening noting that soldiers were risking their lives "to preserve our religion." He felt fully engaged in God's work.

The entreaty for good weather was reproduced in a box on the front page of the *Stars and Stripes*, which irked commanders who lacked Patton's public relations instincts.*

---

*SHAEF censors nevertheless held up release of the prayer to the American press until January 17, 1945.

7

TURNING ABOUT

PATTON SOON WORKED HIS IDIOSYNCRATIC IMPROVE-
ments on O'Neill's prayer for further use. Despite the
frigid weather, his troops began turning about. In the 26th
"Yankee" Division, G Company of the 328th Infantry knew
its moment had come once the 4th Armored and the 80th Divisions were both ordered on their way north. Two men in Company G, Lieutenant Lee M. Otts and Staff Sergeant Bruce
Egger, were keeping diaries that have survived. In a cold fog,
with frost whitening the trees and power lines, just before
noon on the 20th, Otts wrote, the division loaded 2½-ton
trucks, and jeeps, onto long trailer rigs. They proceeded on the
road to Bastogne, bumper-to-bumper, about sixty miles in six
hours, eating their K rations as they motored on. "There were
no stops for nature's calls. We had to stand or sit on the rear
of the truck and just let go." Otts would have appreciated the
"awesomely beautiful" scenery and the steep mountain curves
more if he hadn't been "nervous over what lay before us."

When their convoy slowed through a small town, troops

bargained with onlookers for fresh-baked bread and local wine. "The long loaves of French bread were much better than our K ration crackers." As they paused, a GI hopped off his truck on seeing two pretty girls watching from a porch, and invited himself in for cake and wine. "The trucks pulled out while he was still in the house and we shouted for him as loudly as we could," Egger wrote. "He missed our truck but caught one behind us and joined us on the next stop."

Just before dark they reached Arlon, a city "untouched by the war," it seemed to Egger. The streets were crowded and shop windows illuminated, "bedecked with decorations and Christmas trees." Soldiers were immediately homesick. The closest that some GIs had gotten to replicating a Christmas tree was to hang hand grenades—"pineapples"—on a pine tree sturdy enough to bear the burden. "We all wanted to unload," Lee Otts wrote, "and stay right there." Then, as a cold wind came up and it began to snow, the trucks ground their gears and motored on. Seven miles later, on a wooded hill near a village on the Belgium-Luxembourg border, the convoy halted again and they dug in for the night.

Corporal John MacRae of the 229th Field Artillery Battalion could recall riding a prime mover with winches that drew his 155mm howitzer back from the corner of territory where Belgium, Luxembourg, and Germany intersected. Digging recoil pits daily as they remained within range of the Germans at St. Vith and beyond, they shifted to radio contact and kept firing. His outfit would not lose a weapon but he lost all idea of Christmas, which had happened by the time they rejoined what remained of the 28th Division at Verdun.

To Beatrice, Patton boasted uxoriously from Luxembourg City, "We shoot the works on a chestnut-pulling expedition in the morning. . . . Yesterday I again earned my pay. I visited seven divisions and regrouped an army alone. It was quite a day and I enjoyed it." In brag or from rumor he added, "The Bosch[e] landed a lot of para troops in our uniforms for purpose of murdering Ike, Brad, me, etc." As Stimson had explained in Washington, Patton compared the "situation" to "March 25, 1918," when the last-ditch Hindenburg offensive began in the last war, and he predicted a similar conclusion: "Remember how a tarpon always makes one big flop just before it dies. . . . Destiny sent for me in a hurry when things got tight. Perhaps God saved me for this effort."

Still remote from Bastogne was Maxwell Taylor, absent commander of the 101st Airborne, getting little hard news of the Bulge from the newspapers in Washington. Arriving for a conference at the Pentagon, he first visited the War Room of the Operations Division for an update on the Ardennes. "General," an officer at the reception desk said, "you may not realize it, but your division has just been surrounded." Taylor began trying desperately to get back.

As Bastogne was being encircled and bypassed, Patton's III Corps and XII Corps were still moving north, not quite as quickly as he wanted. In the snow, Ott's platoon was sent six miles off to occupy the Luxembourg border town of Beckerich and secure the bridges to the north. The first shot Otts heard was followed by the cry, "Medic!" One of his men had shot himself in the foot. "Accidents" to get evacuated out would become so frequent that Patton had to convene courts-martial. (It was not "evident," he would admit, "that this eliminated the problem.") "I'll bet there wasn't a man in the outfit," Otts commented sympathetically, "who didn't think about shooting himself at some time or other during combat." In Beckerich he found C Company was already there. Orders were to have a noncom and six men posted at each bridge they had mined. If American troops retreated across, they were to pass over—"but when the first German vehicle or infantryman approached, blow the bridge and run like hell." Lee Otts and Lieutenant Law Lamar of Charlie Company bedded down with their platoons in a nearby stable which had a convenient hayloft above.

Somehow, mail and hot meals followed them—and more snow. "I was not particularly dreaming of a white Christmas this year," Egger wrote. Irving Berlin's sentimental ballad was in its third Christmas season and heard often on Armed Forces Radio. Some months earlier, Churchill's foreign minister, Anthony Eden, had identified to Downing Street the author of the gossipy, informed weekly reports from their embassy in Washington as the distinguished Oxford philosophy don, "Mr. Berlin, of Baltic Jewish extraction." When Clementine Churchill told her husband that a Mr. Berlin was in London, and that the prime minister might like to thank him for his war work, Churchill suggested a lunch, to examine him personally on the Washington scene. At the table Berlin, who didn't seem at all Oxonian, proved vague about American politics and war production. Churchill changed the subject and asked his guest what he thought was the most important thing he had written. "White Christmas," said Berlin. It was not Isaiah, but Irving.

On the 22nd, the 328th Regiment continued in search of the still-unseen enemy. Patton wrote to Beatrice that the Third Army had "progressed on a twenty-mile front to a depth of seven miles." He had "hoped for more but we are in the middle of a snowstorm and there were a lot of demolitions. So I should be content which of course I am not. . . . I think this move of the Third Army is the fastest in history. We moved over a hundred miles starting on the 19th and attacked today all shipshape and Bristol* fashion. With a little luck I will put on a more daring operation just after Xmas." Replacements, he explained with some hasty spelling, were lacking. He combed eight thousand men from his "rear echelons" and made "doeboys" out of clerks and cooks and bandsmen and other service personnel: "If others would do the same [he knew how swollen the support staffs were from Paris to Brussels] we could finish this show in short order." He now had, he noted in his diary, 108 battalions of infantry and artillery in his combined attacking force, with "1,296 guns of 105 [mm] or bigger. I don't see how the Boche can take this much artillery." Yet the Germans bent without buckling, and the advance slowed.

Patton considered Bastogne as good as lost unless he could get armor there by Christmas. South of the town, near Arlon, Major General Hugh Gaffey's 4th Armored Division was moving up ahead of the 26th and 80th Infantry Divisions. On the 22nd, in the snow, a battalion of the 4th Armored lost 33 tanks to tough German artillery units. Patton had urged III Corps commander, Major General John Millikin, to "drive like hell." They were still twelve miles from Bastogne. Despite the cost, Patton goaded him to get close enough to hear the bullets "whistle," and then push on, if he could, through the night.

Decades later, Eisenhower would recall how Patton would telephone with frustrating progress reports from the 4th Armored. "General, I apologize for my slowness. This snow is God-awful. I'm sorry."

"George," Ike would ask, "are you still fighting?"

---

* "Bristol"—an English nautical term for "all in good order."

When Patton conceded he was, Ike answered, "All right, then, that's all I've asked of you."

As the 328th Regiment prepared to move farther on, troops were issued gas masks—not to use, but to carry as obvious evidence that they were not Germans in disguise. No gas masks had been seized from Germans. A light snow fell. Egger packed what he could carry, "an extra pair of drawers, two undershirts, a sweater, four pairs of heavy wool stockings, a scarf, and a pair of [extra] gloves." They were to slog through the snow and slush, following the 1st Battalion, in the lead, until they encountered Germans. A third of the troops, he estimated, "mostly replacements," could not keep up the pace, and some began, riskily, discarding weighty overcoats and overshoes. Egger buckled his boots to his suspenders and tied his coat to his backpack.

By afternoon they reached Redange, where villagers offered them coffee, cookies, and apples, which they ate as they slogged on in the snow. In the fading light, just beyond the village of Grosbus—they were still trudging well above quiet Luxembourg City—they heard gunfire. Egger's 2nd Battalion was ordered to dig defensive positions around Grosbus for the night, and he and a buddy dug a shallow hole which they filled with straw from a nearby barn. He was pleased with himself for not having discarded his heavy overcoat.

Otts's squad had remained in Beckerich awaiting orders. The shops were open. GIs coveted the hot, long loaves of bread right out of the ovens, crowded in for cherry brandy at a tavern, and quaffed "better beer than we had in Metz." French beer was not much. With no chance of lingering there through Christmas, they boarded trucks late in the afternoon to join the battalion, reaching their relocated regimental headquarters "in the rain and freezing cold" two hours before midnight. Near Eschdorf, they were just west of another road to Bastogne.

Colonel William Roberts's command post was a farmhouse a mile below Bastogne. As Hugh M. Cole, the primary historian of the Ardennes battles, put it, "The highway nodal position which made Bastogne so necessary to the Germans also set up a magnetic field for the heterogeneous stragglers, broken infantry, and dismounted tankers heading west. Realizing this, . . . Roberts got permission to gather all stragglers into his command." Nearly a week after the battle had been joined, strays were still emerging from the woods. His motley force, known as Team SNAFU,* became "a reservoir from which regular units drew replacements." Roberts was especially valuable in a sector manned by grounded paratroopers. Earlier in the war, he had been an instructor in tank warfare at the Command and General Staff School at Fort Leavenworth, Kansas. Chutists of the 101st had seldom worked with armor, and "as befitted troops who jumped into thin air"—according to Cole—"they were a little contemptuous of men who fought behind plate steel."

On Troy Middleton's orders early in the Bastogne siege, Roberts had subdivided Combat Command B of his 10th Armored into three combat teams, O'Hara, Cherry, and Desobry, each named, as was the practice, for its commander. They were to scout the likely German approaches to Bastogne. Cherry had been the first to make contact with the Germans. The third and last officer to report was Major William Desobry, who was assigned to hold Noville, a junction six miles to the northeast, and the probable goal of a panzer division. Des-

---

*In laundered vernacular, Situation Normal, All Fouled Up.

obry would have only fifteen Sherman tanks. "You're young," Roberts said in a fatherly fashion, "and by tomorrow morning you'll probably be nervous. Then you'll probably want to pull out. When you begin thinking like that, remember I told you *not* to pull out." To each he offered the same parting remark: "Remember, I'm one of the oldest colonels on the front. . . . I need proper rest. You see that I get it."

As Team Desobry clanked north, it kept encountering stragglers "who told us horror stories about how their units had been overrun." Desobry invited them to join his outfit, "but their physical and mental condition was such that they would be more a burden than a help." Only a platoon from the 9th Armored Division joined up. The others stumbled rearwards.

In treeless Noville in darkness, Desobry holed up in an empty church, and at four in the morning on the nineteenth he heard firing up the road. Soon his men from a patrol sent eastward returned through the fog, with one soldier shot up. German tanks and halftracks were approaching. When the fog lifted at 7:20 a.m., Desobry saw tanks of the 2nd Panzer Division. Fourteen were looking for positions above the low-lying fields. Leading were two halftracks, which his team hit and disabled. He sent engineers to blow them up further—blocking the road—and fired at the tanks to keep them distant. When more tanks appeared, he radioed Roberts for permission to pull back. Told to use his own judgment, Desobry replied, grimly, "I'll get ready to counterattack."

Roberts ordered a battalion of the 101st led by Lieutenant Colonel James La Prade to the rescue, and firing went on for two hours. As they took prisoners, one gave Desobry the Hitler outstretched-arm salute. Desobry had seen *The Great Dictator* and thought, "This is getting like a Charlie Chaplin movie." But the reality was not comic. They were severely outnumbered, and he told his men, "OK, good try—but let's pull back into the town." In Noville they hurriedly reorganized with the more senior La Prade in command. A few minutes later, an .88 shell exploded near their command post. Among the dead was La Prade.

Desobry and three other wounded were loaded on litters in a medic jeep to return to Bastogne but the driver soon lost his way and encountered the *Panzergrenadiers*. As the Germans wanted nothing to do with the inconvenience of taking casualties as prisoners, they waved the jeep on. When the other wounded died en route and the driver blundered again, Desobry spent Christmas in a field hospital—a German one. Yet the improvised defense, put under Major Robert F. Harwick of the 101st, held for two days, a delay that kept the Bastogne perimeter below Noville intact.

Team O'Hara's patrol out to the east was led by Lieutenant John Drew Devereaux of the acting family associated with the Barrymores. Before putting on his uniform he had been on Broadway in the long-running *Life with Father*. The village of Wardin was still fogged in, but once people saw the jeep was American, they emerged from their houses and warned that there were Germans all about. "Keep to your cellars," said Devereaux, "but don't be afraid." As the fog began lifting he drove forward and spotted what appeared to be an American halftrack and armored car. "My God, those are Krauts!" said the GI next to him. The vehicles may have been American but the occupants were not. One fired from the halftrack at the jeep, rocking it. Devereaux made a sharp turn and raced back toward Wardin. "The Germans are coming!" he shouted. "Get back to your cellars!" Outdistancing the slower armor, Devereaux gunned toward Bastogne with the rest of Team O'Hara.

8

"NUTS!"

"FOR ONCE, WE THINK OURSELVES A THOUSAND TIMES better off than you at home," a panzer officer with the volatile surname of Rockhammer wrote ebulliently to his wife on the 22nd. "We shall throw those arrogant big-mouthed apes from the New World into the sea. They will not get into our Germany. . . . If we are to save everything that is sweet and lovely in our lives, we must be ruthless at this decisive hour in our struggle." On the northern shoulder of the Bulge, St. Vith, finally in *Wehrmacht* hands, seemed to open up a path, if precious fuel held out, through Liège to Antwerp. Bastogne, the key road junction in the Bulge still in Allied hands, led to the Meuse.

After the war, von Manteuffel confided under interrogation, "We wanted St. Vith very badly; in fact it was vital to us in the first days of the attack. If St. Vith had fallen earlier, we would have been able to move on much more rapidly. . . . by preventing a defence line along the Amblève and Salm rivers. . . . St. Vith was much more important to us than Bastogne at that time, and those four days of waiting in front of St. Vith were of great disadvantage."

With the town taken, more Germans became available to surround Bastogne. Although artillery could reach every point within the town, the western perimeter remained thinly manned as more troops were diverted toward the Meuse. On the morning of December 22, General Heinrich von Lüttwitz determined that he would end the standoff by bluffing that he could take Bastogne with the forces at his disposal. He sent a major, a captain, and two enlisted men under cover of a white flag to the company command post of the 327th Glider Infantry. Major Alvin Jones, its operations officer, hurried to the CP to receive them. Helmuth Henke of Lüttwitz's Panzer Lehr Division had been in the import business before the war and spoke passable English. "We are *parlementaires* [bearers of a flag of truce]" Henke said, producing a letter in English and German. "We want to talk to your commanding general."

While their men waited, the German officers, accepting blindfolds, were jeeped to Marvie, a village on the southeast perimeter facing Panzer Lehr. With the delivery of the ultimatum came the added persuasion of a cessation of firing, creating fast-spreading if illogical rumors that the Germans intended to surrender. In any case, there was sudden calm to exploit. Some troops used the break to shave, others to risk a visit to a latrine.

The peripatetic McAuliffe was about to leave Marvie to congratulate men manning a roadblock who had repelled an enemy attack. As the Germans stood waiting, Major Jones handed the bilingual message to Colonel Norman Moore. "What does it say, Ned?" McAuliffe asked as Moore scanned the English text.

"They want you to surrender," Moore explained.*

"Aw, nuts!" said McAuliffe with some irritation at being bothered with what seemed an obvious absurdity. Nevertheless, he read the English text of the message:

To the U.S.A. Commander of the encircled town of Bastogne.

The fortune of war is changing. This time the U.S.A. forces in and near Bastogne have been encircled by strong German armored units. More German armored units have crossed the river Ourthe . . . , have taken Marche and reached St. Hubert. . . . Libramont is in German hands.

There is only one possibility to save the encircled U.S.A. troops from total annihilation: that is the honorable surrender of the encircled town. In order to think it over, a term of two hours will be granted beginning with the presentation of this note. If this proposal should be rejected, one German Artillery Corps and six heavy A.A. Battalions are ready to annihilate the U.S.A. troops in and near Bastogne. The order for [resuming] firing will be given immediately after this two hours' term.

All the serious civilian losses caused by this artillery fire would not correspond with the well-known American humanity.

—*The German Commander*

McAuliffe let the paper drop to the floor. "Nuts!" he said again. He walked off a few paces, then returned and sat down. Several senior officers gathered round. "Well," McAuliffe

---

*The exchange differs slightly from account to account. For example "you" becomes "us."

began, pondering how to phrase his refusal, "I don't know what to tell them."

Colonel Harry Kinnard, his G-3, suggested, "That first crack you made would be hard to beat, General."

"What was that?"

"You said 'Nuts!'"

It was, then, not so much as in decades since, a breezy American term for madness. In England a century earlier, *nut* had become Cockney slang for *head*. A person could be "off his nut"—drunk or insane. Americans had improved on it, turning it into an expletive.

McAuliffe asked for a blank piece of paper and wrote, curtly, "To the German Commander: Nuts! A. C. McAuliffe, American Commander." He called over Colonel Joseph H. ("Bud") Harper of the 327th Glider Infantry Regiment, who had been summoned by radio. McAuliffe handed him the message.

"Would you see that it's delivered?"

"I'll deliver it myself, General," said Harper, looking at the message with a surge of pride. "It will be a lot of fun."

"Don't go into their lines," McAuliffe warned.

The waiting Germans were blindfolded again. Harper told Major Henke to deliver the official response: "I will stick it in your hand."

Henke was puzzled. "Is that reply negative or affirmative? If it is the latter, I will negotiate further."

"The reply is decidedly not affirmative," Harper explained, "and if you continue this foolish attack, your losses will be tremendous." Without further comment he had the two officers returned by jeep to the outpost where the other Germans were waiting with their white flag. As they prepared to leave, Harper elaborated, "If you don't know what 'Nuts!' means, in plain English it is the same as 'Go to Hell!' And I will tell you something else: if you continue to attack, we will kill every goddam German who tries to break into this city."

Blindfolds removed, the emissaries sprang to attention before departing. The air had turned sharp with frost. Henke, who survived the war, recalled, "I told the American officer what I told every soldier I took prisoner—'May you make it back to your homeland safe and sound.'"

"Go to hell!" Harper said impatiently.

"We will kill many Americans," Captain Henke warned. "This is war." All four Germans turned smartly and trod down the snow-covered road. By three in the afternoon they reached Baron von Lüttwitz's headquarters in the Château Roumont.

Although German firing resumed, McAuliffe's four-letter response quickly echoed across Bastogne. Spirits rose. Almost certainly with no pun intended, although the expletive had alternative meanings, Sergeant Bill True of F Company, 506th Parachute Infantry, told his friend Otto May, "That guy has balls!" Patton's men were coming, they knew. They had to hold on until then, although the edges of their lines around the town were fraying. And it seemed as cold as in the days when, as a kid, Bill True got up winter mornings to deliver the *Omaha Herald*.

At a press conference on December 22, when the Bulge was nearly one week along, President Roosevelt turned back any comment on the German offensive. Asked about previous victory projections, he conceded that the end was "not yet in sight." At one point just before Christmas, concerned about increasing casualties and the lengthening of the war, he called in Secretary Stimson and Major General Leslie Groves, who oversaw the supersecret "Manhattan Project." Could an atomic bomb, he asked, be rushed into readiness if urgently needed to crush the Ardennes salient? The president did not realize that even had a crude nuclear device been deployable, it would have been useless as a tactical weapon, spreading radioactive fallout in every direction. Groves advised that no trigger mechanism yet existed, but that he hoped the first bomb would be ready by summer—perhaps in August. "If we can't test it first, the mechanism might not go off. Then the Germans might find out how it works." Despite later racist allegations, the atomic bomb was not being withheld for use against Japan.

Lüttwitz's Panzer Lehr Division, augmented by artillery, remained the primary force to deal with the siege while other troops pushed on toward St. Hubert, only twenty miles from the Meuse. Despite the scornful rejection of his ultimatum, he expected Bastogne to run out of food and fuel soon after Christmas.

In Luxembourg City on the morning of the 23rd, General Patton sought out the ancient Roman Catholic chapel in the *Fondation Pescatore,* the massive, steepled, castlelike structure in which he now used a corner as his headquarters. It was an old people's home. Under the crucifix above the altar, Patton, although an Episcopalian, removed his helmet with its three stars, sank to his knees, and prayed earnestly for the Christmastime success of his troops. God in Patton's quirky concept was the ultimate commanding general:

Sir, this is Patton talking. The last fourteen days have been straight hell. Rain, snow, more rain, more snow—and I'm beginning to wonder what's going on in Your headquarters. Whose side are You on, anyway?

For three years my chaplains have been explaining that this is a religious war. This, they tell me, is the Crusades all over again, except that we're riding tanks instead of chargers. They insist that we are here to annihilate the Germans and the godless Hitler so that religious freedom may return to Europe. Up until now I have gone along with them, for You have given us Your unreserved cooperation. Clear skies and a calm sea in Africa made the landings highly successful and helped us to eliminate Rommel.* Sicily was comparatively easy and You supplied excellent weather for our armored dash across France, the greatest military victory that You have thus far allowed me. You have often given me excellent guidance in difficult command decisions and You have led German units into traps that made their elimination fairly simple.

But now, You've changed horses in midstream. You seem to have given von Rundstedt every break in the book and frankly, he's been beating the hell out of us. My army is neither trained nor equipped for winter warfare. And as You know this weather is more suitable for Eskimos than for southern cavalrymen.

But now, Sir, I can't help but feel that I have offended You in some way. That suddenly You have lost all sympathy for our cause. That You are throwing in with von Rundstedt and his paper-hanging-god [, Hitler]. You know without me telling You that our situation is desperate. Sure, I can tell my staff that everything is going according

---

*Presumably God understood that Field Marshal Erwin Rommel had commanded the *Afrika Korps*.

to plan, but there's no use telling You that my 101st Airborne is holding out against tremendous odds in Bastogne, and that this continual storm is making it impossible to supply them even from the air. I've sent Hugh Gaffey, one of my ablest generals, with his 4th Armored Division, north toward that all-important road center to relieve the encircled garrison and he's finding Your weather more difficult than he is to the Krauts.

I don't like to complain unreasonably, but my soldiers from the Meuse to Echternach are suffering tortures of the damned. Today I visited several hospitals, all full of frostbite cases, and the wounded are dying in the fields because they cannot be brought back for medical care.

But this isn't the worst of the situation. Lack of visibility, continued rains, have completely grounded my air force. My technique of battle calls for close-in fighter-bomber support, and if my planes can't fly, how can I use them as aerial artillery? Not only is this a deplorable situation, but, worse yet, my reconnaissance planes haven't been in the air for fourteen days and I haven't the faintest idea of what is going on behind the German lines.

Damn it, Sir, I can't fight a shadow. Without Your cooperation from a weather standpoint I am deprived of accurate disposition of the German armies and how in hell can I be intelligent in my attack? All of this probably sounds unreasonable to You, but I have lost all patience with Your chaplains who insist that this is a typical Ardennes winter, and that I must have faith.

Faith and patience be damned! You have just got to make up Your mind whose side You're on. You must come to my assistance, so that I may dispatch the entire German Army as a birthday present to Your Prince of Peace.

Sir, I have never been an unreasonable man; I am not going to ask You for the impossible. I do not even insist upon a miracle, for all I request is four days of clear weather.

Give me four clear days so that my planes can fly, so that my fighter-bombers can bomb and strafe, so that my reconnaissance may pick out targets for my magnificent artillery. Give me four days of sunshine to dry this blasted mud, so that my tanks roll, so that ammunition and rations may be taken to my hungry, ill-equipped infantry. I need these four days to send von Rundstedt and his godless army to their Valhalla. I am sick of this unnecessary butchery of American youth, and in exchange for four days of fighting weather. I will deliver You enough Krauts to keep Your bookkeepers months behind their work.

Amen.

9

"ONE MORE SHOPPING DAY"

WITH NO LIKELIHOOD OF A SURRENDER AT BAStogne, Rundstedt ratcheted up a more serious siege that would drain resources from any further advance toward the Meuse. Manteuffel employed a fresh division, the 15th *Panzergrenadiers,* just arrived from Italy, where a winter stalemate continued. Both generals knew that Patton's Third Army was intent on relieving Bastogne from the south. There wasn't much more time to make that effort useless.

That Saturday, December 23, from the command post in Bastogne Colonel Kinnard anxiously telephoned Middleton's VIII Corps headquarters at Neufchâteau, "It is getting rather sticky around here. They [the 4th Armored] must keep coming. The enemy has attacked all along the south [perimeter] and some tanks are through and running around our area. Request you inform 4th Armored Division of our situation and ask them to put on all possible pressure." One of McAuliffe's staff radioed the 4th Armored command on his own, "There is only one more shopping day before Christmas!"

Hugh Gaffey's vehicles were finding it hard going, and to allay Patton's impatience, Major General John Millikin transferred to Gaffey two battalions of the 80th Division's 318th Infantry. Fighting south of Bastogne was costly on both sides in men and machines. Ambushes occurred from the cover of thick woods. Riskily riding the backs of tanks, German infantrymen were toppled into the snow by concealed small-arms fire.

Captain John T. Prior, the battalion surgeon for the 10th Armored, had more than a hundred serious cases and dwindling supplies. He checked on the 101st's medical situation, which he knew was even worse. Since its clearing hospital had been attacked and destroyed almost on arrival, all the division had were glorified aid stations. Prior found the senior surviving regimental surgeon, Major Douglas Davidson of the 502nd Parachute Infantry, at an improvised hospital in a former Belgian army barracks compound. In the riding hall, Prior recalled, "on the dirt riding floor, were six hundred paratroop litter cases. I cannot recall the number of walking wounded or psychiatric casualties. These patients were only being sustained, as were mine. I did see a paratroop chaplain (armed with a pistol and shoulder holster) moving among the dying."

Davidson would try, on Christmas Eve, to arrange a truce for medical evacuation, chancing the German lines himself with a white flag. According to Captain Prior the request "was refused by the ranking German medical officer." Responding to radioed appeals, eleven gliders were towed under hazardous conditions to the drop zone with doctors, medics, and medical supplies aboard. They emerged through the fog soon after and crash-landed safely inside the perimeter. Until then the only anesthesia available had been whiskey, usually cognac. The harried medical staff was grateful for the glider teams; still, none of the urgent cases could be evacuated.

Near Eupen, just above the northernmost shoulder of the Bulge, the First Army, following traditional rules of war, executed by firing squad German parachutists captured in American uniforms and wearing appropriated GI dog tags. Although they had been close to the huge Stavelot dump that held over two million barrels of fuel, none of them had known. One German officer asked for a pistol to commit suicide, "and thus held fast," a First Army diarist wrote, "to his strange and outworn conception of honor. We shall cordially accommodate him." According to Hodges's diary, "The prisoners' last request was to hear Christmas carols, sung by a group of German women prisoners." (Several nurses had been interned, but only on January 25, 1945, did Sergeant Clifford Laski of the 3rd Regiment, 2nd Infantry Division report about one POW, "It wasn't until she took her helmet off and revealed those long locks of hair that we knew her to be a woman, because she wasn't particularly chesty.") At least eighteen of Skorzeny's men were shot at Henri-Chapelle in Belgium, northwest of Eupen. Moments before the twelve riflemen fired at targets pinned on the chests of the condemned men, officer cadet Günter Billing shouted shrilly, *"Lang lebe unser Führer!"** Only three Skorzeny jeep teams would return to their lines intact.

As Patton left the chapel in Luxembourg, he did not yet know that his prayer seemed to have been anticipated. The

---

* "Long live . . ."

skies were clearing, Bradley recalled. "Each morning our gloom had deepened as the Ninth Air Force's youthful meteorologist opened the daily briefing with his dismally repetitious report. And each morning [Lieutenant General Hoyt] Vandenberg, in a chair next to mine, pulled his head a little tighter into his leather flying jacket. On more than 100 socked-in airfields from Scotland to Brussels, an Allied Air Force of over 4,000 planes waited for the end of von Rundstedt's conspiracy with the weather."

Finally that morning, the Ninth Air Force war room received a radioed report of cloudless skies coming their way from the west. IX Troop Carrier Command loaded transports to try Bastogne once the overcast lifted. Soon the skies streamed with their contrails. Some of the color-coded parachutes drifted short and supplied the Germans with an unexpected early Christmas, and enemy antiaircraft 88s picked off some of the slow, overloaded Douglas C-47s, the commercial DC-3. Nineteen crash-landed, including one christened the *Ain't Misbehavin'*, which belly-flopped at Savy, northeast of Bastogne. With powerful big-bellied P-47 Thunderbolts flying cover, 1,200 support and supply sorties were flown across the humpbacked front.

As fighter-bombers hammered German vehicles, Patton telephoned General Millikin impatiently—and unreasonably. "There's too much piddling around!" he complained safely from Luxembourg City. The 4th Armored was still far from Bastogne. Tough German resistance at Chaumont disabled eleven American tanks. "Bypass these towns and clear them up later," Patton ordered. "Tanks can operate on this ground now."

Buoyantly, Patton credited his chaplain for the clearing weather. "God damn!" he exulted. "That O'Neill sure did some potent praying. Get him up here, I want to pin a medal on him." General Gaffey of the 4th Armored observed wryly in his diary, "It would appear that the prayer written and put out by the Chaplain of the Third Army has been answered." Happily, if prematurely, Patton radioed to McAuliffe on the morning of the 24th, referring to Gaffey's tanks, "Xmas Eve present coming. Hold on." But another Christmas gift had already begun to arrive, beginning at 1:30 p.m. on the 23rd. Townspeople hearing the throb of aircraft engines climbed out of their cellars to wave.

The first resupply planes made it through to a field west of Bastogne cleared and lighted just enough for a drop zone. Paratroopers looked for food and fuel and ammo drifting down, but the first chutes to reach them disappointingly carried only personnel-pathfinders to lay down spotting zones. The colorful chutes followed. Their most precious cargo was artillery shells. Strict rationing—six rounds daily per mortar— had kept artillerymen from targeting anything but the most crucial objectives.

By afternoon on the 24th, 241 aircraft had dropped 236 tons of supplies, including 24,406 K rations. A brief spoiling *Luftwaffe* raid did little to disrupt the unloading. Watching from nearby foxholes, men cheered the early Christmas. Troops could now call in reports of approaching enemy tanks with coordinates, and in twenty minutes P-47s were hammering the Germans. Other fighter-bombers set afire tanks and halftracks that were targets of opportunity. Airmen did not expect the "Siberian high" to last, but were making the most of it—sometimes in too much of a hurry.

That morning Bruce Egger saw a flight of American bombers returning from a mission. "One plane was on fire but was still in formation as the flight passed from our view."

American aircraft had been rare sights until then, and one GI in his platoon impulsively shot at an out-of-range P-47. Soldiers often fired angrily at American aircraft when they gunned and bombed mistakenly what seemed to be enemy targets miles away. Malmédy was hit by pilots confusing the town with St. Vith. Once in flames, it attracted more bombers and was struck three times from December 23 through Christmas Day. The 30th Division lost 35 soldiers and the town 125 civilians. Men of the 30th called the erratically zealous Ninth Air Force bitterly, "the American Luftwaffe." It was nothing new. Since D-Day, hundreds of troops had been killed by "friendly fire," including a lieutenant general, Lesley McNair, one of Marshall's key deputies.

In Luxembourg, south of the 4th Division's command post at Junglinster, an ambulance of the 5th Medical Battalion, carrying casualties from Echternach to the north, was shot up and set afire near Gonderange by a P-47. When the ambulance crashed into a tree, killing all aboard, American infantrymen angrily shot down the plane. The pilot survived. A squadron of sleek twin-boom P-38s strafed the placid Belgian village of Buissonville, which the 2nd Armored Division had reached. The planes had been called off, but too late.

More often, the fighter-bombers found authentic targets, even St. Vith itself. "The worst of it," General Sepp Dietrich deplored, "is that those damned Jabos* don't distinguish between generals and anyone else—it was terrible!" On the day before Christmas, Allied planes flew over five thousand sorties and the *Luftwaffe* 1,088—an effort that eroded German air strength and left a dwindling pool of experienced air-

---

*Fighter-bombers (*Jagd-bomber*).

The New York Times headlines the positive and the negative after a week of the Bulge, December 23, 1944.

Courtesy of *The New York Times*

Volksgrenadiers receive an inspection in the snowy Ardennes forest before jumping off against American forces, mid-December 1944.

U.S. Army from captured German film

Unidentified American infantry move to the front, through the Kinkelter Woods in Belgium, December 20, 1944.

U.S. Army photo

Lieutenant Colonel Jochen Peiper's men after their breakthrough, 13 kilometers from Malmedy.

U.S. Army from captured German film

"Hinter der letzten Schlacht dieses Krieg steht under Sieg"—Behind the last battle of this war stands our Victory—a slogan daubed on a slate wall in Troisvierges, Luxembourg, probably on December 20, 1944.

U.S. Army from captured German film

A GI runs for cover as a buddy lies dead at his feet in the snow. Ardennes, December 1944.

U.S. Army Signal Corps

Soldiers of the 3rd Fallschirm-Jager Division pick trophies and combat gear from dead Americans lying in the snow. Especially prized were boots and rations.

U.S. Army from captured German film

Ernest Hemingway, bundled up in two coats, with Major General Raymond Burton at the command post in Junglinster, December 20, 1944.

U.S. Army Signal Corps

Marlene Dietrich singing for American troops in a barn near the front lines. Shelling nearby did not interrupt her performance.

U.S. Army Signal Corps

Wind-whipped snow near the Stavelot fuel dump, December 1944.

Signal Corps photo, USAMI

Vehicles of the 99th Division loading for Elsenborn on the second day of the Bulge.

Signal Corps photo, USAMHI

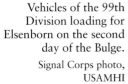

Paratroop infantry of the 101st Airborne Division trudging in the snow toward Bastogne from the trucks that took them eastward, December 19, 1944.

U.S. Army Signal Corps

American prisoners being marched to the German rear, December 20, 1944, under the watchful gaze of panzer troops in a Tiger tank.

U.S. Army from captured German film

American anti-aircraft gunners watch the vapor trails of aircraft flying escort for cargo planes heading for Bastogne just before Christmas, and German planes trying to intercept the airlift.

U.S. Army Signal Corps

One of 241 C-47s of the IX Troop Carrier Command
parachuting supplies for Bastogne on the western perimeter of
the town, December 23, 1944.

U.S. Army Signal Corps

A supply convoy unloading in still-snowy Bastogne after
the breaking of the siege.

U.S. Army Signal Corps

HEADQUARTERS 101ST AIRBORNE DIVISION
Office of the Division Commander

24 December 1944

What's Merry about all this, you ask? We're fighting - it's cold we aren't home. All true but what has the proud Eagle Division accomplished with its worthy comrades the 10th Armored Division, the 705th Tank Destroyer Battalion and all the rest? Just this: We have stopped cold everything that has been thrown at us from the North, East, South and West. We have identifications from four German Panzer Divisions, two German Infantry Divisions and one German Parachute Division. These units, spearheading the last desperate German lunge, were headed straight west for key points when the Eagle Division was hurriedly ordered to stem the advance. How effectively this was done will be written in history; not alone in our Division's glorious history but in World history. The Germans actually did surround us, their radios blared our doom. Their Commander demanded our surrender in the following impudent arrogance:

December 22nd 1944

"To the U. S. A. Commander of the encircled town of Bastogne.

The fortune of war is changing. This time the U. S. A. forces in and near Bastogne have been encircled by strong German armored units. More German armored units have crossed the river Ourthe near Ortheuville, have taken Marche and reached St. Hubert by passing through Hompres-Sibret-Tillet. Libramont is in German hands.

There is only one possibility to save the encircled U. S. A. Troops from total annihilation: that is the honorable surrender of the encircled town. In order to think it over a term of two hours will be granted beginning with the presentation of this note.

If this proposal should be rejected one German Artillery Corps and six heavy A. A. Battalions are ready to annihilate the U. S. A. Troops in and near Bastogne. The order for firing will be given immediately after this two hour's term.

All the serious civilian losses caused by this Artillery fire would not correspond with the well known American humanity.

The German Commander"

The German Commander received the following reply:

22 December 1944

"To the German Commander:

N U T S !

The American Commander"

Allied Troops are counterattacking in force. We continue to hold Bastogne. By holding Bastogne we assure the success of the Allied Armies. We know that our Division Commander, General Taylor, will say: "Well Done! "

We are giving our country and our loved ones at home a worthy Christmas present and being privileged to take part in this gallant feat of arms are truly making for ourselves a Merry Christmas.

/s/ A. C. McAULIFFE
/t/   McAULIFFE
Commanding.

McAuliffe's Christmas message to the 101st Airborne.
U.S. Army photo

An improvised mass on Christmas Day in Bastogne, with a real Christmas tree and local ornaments.

U.S. Army Signal Corps

Christmas dinner at headquarters in Bastogne. From left to right: Colonel William Roberts, Lieutenant Colonel Ned Moore, Brigadier Generals Gerald Higgins and Anthony McAuliffe, Colonel Thomas Sherburne, Jr., Lieutenant Colonels Harry Kinnard and Paul Danahy, and Colonel Curtis D. Renfro.

U.S. Army Signal Corps

German graves in Wiltz, Luxembourg. German-style crosses are atop each marker.

U.S. Army Signal Corps

The first "Cobra" of the 37th Tank Battalion of the 4th Armored Division begins to enter Bastogne from the south on December 26, 1944.

U.S. Army Signal Corps

Major General Maxwell Taylor, commander of the 101st but absent in Washington until Christmas, on return greets his temporary replacement in Bastogne, Brigadier General McAuliffe.

U.S. Army Signal Corps

A warning sign in Bastogne just after Christmas that did not fit the circumstances.

U.S. Army Signal Corps

"Aus die Traum"—the dream is over—perhaps not written by the grenadier in Rochefort, Belgium, who is sadly viewing the wreckage on which the confession is daubed.

U.S. Army from captured German film

Bradley, Eisenhower, and Patton in Bastogne early in 1945, on Eisenhower's first visit after the Bulge battles. Despite Patton's garb, it is obvious that the weather has moderated.

U.S. Army Signal Corps

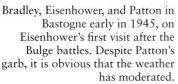

men. When darkness fell on the southern flank, Major General Ludwig Heilmann of the 5th Paratroop Division reported, "One could see from Bastogne back to the *Westwall,* a single torchlight procession of burning vehicles." Their own.

In St. Vith, held by the 18th *Volksgrenadiers,* Lieutenant Rolf-Helmut Schröder looked for safety from the first American strikes of the morning and thought unhappily, "This is not going to be easy." A veteran of the Eastern Front, he had never been under heavy air attack. His unit began to withdraw under a replacement colonel newly arrived from quiet Norway, who, Schröder realized, wore a tunic bare of combat decorations because he hadn't earned any. During another American attack the green colonel panicked. Seen slipping away, he explained, unconvincingly, "Schröder, I'm afraid my foot is playing up."

Although Skorzeny's commandos had largely been captured, killed, or inserted into improvised infantry squads, opportunistic Germans still found ways to deceive the enemy. The many American dead continued to furnish uniforms in which to masquerade, and on Christmas Eve an assault group of the 2nd Panzers in seized American garb struck at the Belgian village of Humain, well to the northwest of Bastogne, on the road toward Celles and the Meuse. Burned-out tanks and half-tracks of both sides lay athwart its path. The column moved on toward Buissonville, where two American tanks guarded a bridge over which the Havrenne road entered the village. A German officer in American uniform went ahead and brazenly ordered the tankers to return to their bivouac—which they did. Then four Panther tanks crossed the bridge, only to be identified and driven back by heavy antitank fire, losing a fifth Panther which came to their aid.

*   *   *

Bruce Egger's 2nd Battalion was in a task force to recover the high ground near Eschdorf and establish a bridgehead across the Sure River. As they moved forward, the division's 104th Regiment began taking fire from German tanks blocking any further movement toward Bastogne. The battalion dug in near Weishof, a group of buildings hardly a village. Egger slept with his boots on in case the enemy attacked. Some now regretted having shed the weight of what had seemed to be surplus blankets. Fortunately—or unfortunately—the dead often had blankets and overcoats.

To dig foxholes, Otts and his company had to clear a coating of ice covering eight to ten inches of snow. Some were blasted rather than dug. Foxholes meant safety, but they were also hazardous from above and below. Shell bursts in the trees rained down branches and metal fragments. "We slept with our canteens in our foxholes next to us to keep the water from freezing and bursting them. The holes were more comfortable than they had been before the snow—at least they were not full of water. Two men with eight blankets could sleep very comfortably. The only difficulty was getting the eight blankets. We would put one shelter half [half a small tent] and our raincoat with about three blankets below us and the other five blankets and another shelter half (if we had one) over us." When GIs were desperate for protection from shrapnel or weather and had no logs, a frozen "stiff" would do. There was no shortage of bodies in the Bulge.

On the morning before Christmas, Sergeant Egger could not see from ground level what was going on as forward elements of his task force began to move toward Eschdorf, but he heard mortar, artillery, and small-arms fire. When F Company climbed a hill toward the Germans, they were silhouetted against the snow and drew fire from machine guns and a camouflaged 88-mm close to a farmhouse. The GIs took cover—all but two who crawled forward with bazookas and knocked out, from up close, the .88 and a tank beside the farmhouse.

Once the farmhouse area was neutralized, troops could get warm inside and heat up frozen C rations. Easy and Fox companies dug in on the edge of Eschdorf. They had a house—an unexpected Christmas bonus. "It was Christmas Eve," Lee Otts wrote, "and we sat around on the floor in our house, each man with his own thoughts of home and dreading what Christmas Day might bring. I had dozed off for about an hour when we were awakened and told to 'saddle up' and hit the road." Lieutenant John Schell of the 328th Regiment of the 26th Division walked toward Eschdorf with his platoon under a starry sky with a battalion of eight hundred men, unaware that a German regiment—three times their number—lay ahead. Spotting a sentry on the moonlit road, Schell realized they could not evade him. He fired, and the unseen Germans well behind the fallen sentry poured in a barrage that pinned down the Americans.

They crawled toward nearby barns. The wounded lay on dirt floors in the darkness and called pitifully for their mothers. A grenade blew out a room and sprayed shrapnel into Schell's side. Another officer dragging a field telephone cranked it and called back to regimental headquarters for supporting artillery fire. "They said it was too dangerous," Schell recalled. "It's that or we're going to be killed," the officer on the phone pleaded. It was already Christmas Day when the requested fire poured in and the Germans fell back. Schell had promised the immobile wounded that he wouldn't leave without them, but there were no medics, no stretchers. Half the platoon failed to return. "That was the very worst day of my life, bar none," he remembered.

* * *

As Patton's troops closed in on Bastogne, the German coun-teroffensive was reaching its limits. By Christmas Eve tanks from the 2nd Panzer Division, low on fuel, had reached Celles, only a few miles from a bend in the Meuse. Sixty miles from the start line on December 16, Celles would be as far as the Bulge would extend—but for a single captured vehicle. On the right bank of the Meuse, at Dinant, a German patrol in a jeep and American uniforms blew up on striking a mined daisy chain concealed in the rock defilade. No one survived. Although German radio taunted GIs that they were only clinging to enemy flanks, the Germans had been effectively thwarted. In Luxembourg City, Bradley told Hansen confi-dently, as if he were not largely an observer, "We're safe as long as we hold the shoulders."

The bulk of the 2nd Panzers were on the road northwest from Bastogne beyond Marche-en-Famenne. Below Marche was Bande, a center of resistance during the German occupa-tion which paid for its role by having its houses along the main highway burned in reprisal. Students from the Bastogne semi-nary had been evacuated to Bande by the stocky, dark-haired Abbé Jean-Baptiste Musty, who celebrated high mass in the village church late that morning. Interrupting the service, Himmler's dreaded SD *(Sicherheitsdienst)* agents accompany-ing the 2nd Panzers to ensure their discipline seized four of Musty's students, marching the surprised seminarians to a local sawmill along with sixty-six other men and boys of the village. Nazi reprisals were not over.

Musty tried to secure their release but was refused entrance to the Rulkin sawmill. The anxious wife of a Bande innkeeper arrived next, carrying two overcoats for her husband, René

Tournay, and their son. She felt certain all seventy hostages would be taken to Germany as slave laborers. An officer warning her off promised nevertheless to deliver the coats if she would procure some cognac for him. Mme. Tournay pleaded that she had none, but the SD officer claimed he knew better. "People like you always have cognac hidden somewhere. I know, I'm in the Gestapo."

She returned with three bottles of champagne as a substitute, asking as she handed them over whether he would free her family, and also her nephew, Xavier Tournay.

"People don't bargain with me," he snapped. "I'm not a Jew."

Inside the sawmill another officer had discovered that one of his hostages, Armand Toussaint, was a farmer. "Farmers always have wine," he contended. "We need some for our Christmas celebration. If you bring me twenty bottles, I'll free you and your son."

Toussaint hurried back to his farmhouse, where a *Wehrmacht* officer was already billeted. "Don't go back to the sawmill," the German warned. "Let me go. I'll fix things up."

He soon returned, rather glum. "There's nothing I can do for you, Monsieur," he said. "Those people down there are strangers. You'd better take them the wine."

To Toussaint's surprise, when he delivered the bottles demanded, he and his son were released. The other captives were separated into two groups. Older men were left in the mill. Thirty-three younger men were marched to the rear of the Rulkin house near the mill and lined up in three rows. Guards went from one to another of the captives, taking all their possessions—watches, pocketbooks, handkerchiefs, and even rosaries. They were ordered to raise their arms over their heads, and cross them, then march down the highway to the

Café de la Poste at the entrance to the village. Again they were lined up in three rows, facing the road. Six soldiers guarded them while an officer left to reconnoiter a burned-out house next to the inn.

The afternoon was now darkening into Christmas Eve. Snow began falling in heavy flakes, whitening the bare heads and the clothes of the anxious young men. At a signal a stocky sergeant who seemed middle-aged put his hand on the shoulder of the last man in the third row and led him into the shell of the house. The other hostages were startled by a shot. Emerging, the SS sergeant tapped the next man. The others must have now realized that they were going to be murdered one by one.

"Let's try and escape," whispered Leon Praille, a tall, sturdy twenty-one year-old. "We'll attack the guards. It's our only chance." No one moved. Praille watched as another Belgian student was seized and shot in the neck with a machine pistol, the sergeant not even bothering to take him inside. The corpse was kicked into the burned-out cellar of the ruin. Counting ahead, Praille realized that he would be the twenty-first. When he felt a hand on his shoulder he looked down at the German sergeant. The brutal killings had unnerved him; he was shaken and crying. As they neared the doorway, Praille, summoning up the courage of desperation, struck the much smaller man in the face, knocking him to the ground. Running up the road and darting across it, Praille jumped a hedge, waded across an icy stream, and disappeared into the dusk.

Too preoccupied to chase after Praille, the other guards stolidly continued the massacre without him. Several of the thirty-two bullet-ridden bodies in the dark cellar twitched. A Gestapo officer emptied the clip of his pistol into the mass.

As snow began to cover the corpses in the roofless ruin, the six Germans explored nearby house wreckage for planks they could rip up to cover the bodies. As they did, an SS officer came by, a Lieutenant Spann from Manteuffel's army, who had discovered that one of the captives at the mill was the elderly owner of the house in which he was billeted, a Monsieur Godfraind. Spann looked away from the gruesome business and hoped that his "host" was not in the cellar.

At the mill he pleaded for Godfraind's release. The SD men brought him out, telling Spann sardonically to take their hostage home for Christmas. "Be happy your husband is alive," Spann told Mme. Godfraind on returning. Explaining only a little of what he saw, he added, "I am very sad." Officer lodgers close by asked him to join their Christmas festivities. They had lots of looted drink. He shook his head.

Late on January 11, 1945, a British unit recaptured the village. The Abbé took them to the ruin of the Bertrand house. Three Tommies pulled away the planks, still heavy with snow. An officer looking on turned to his sergeant. "I want every man brought down here. I want them to see what kind of enemy we're fighting." A photo survives of Musty, bareheaded and in black cassock, identifying the bodies of his four students, with Praille, the survivor, towering over him.

Stephan Roth, a German soldier of nineteen, wounded and captured on September 2 by a Free French unit armed with motley weapons from two wars, plus pitchforks and spades, spent Christmas Eve in a prison camp in Normandy run by the British. As he was prisoner 625411 and his enclosure tented 12,000, many more POW camps had obviously sprouted across France. Few were run as indulgently. Although guards were anxious about what the Germans referred to lightly as the

Rundstedt Offensive, Roth knew that "it was already five minutes after twelve." Christmas was coming, but not victory. Recognizing that, a German and an Austrian in his company of about 500 scrounged a small evergreen while beyond the barbed wire with their labor detail, set it up in their squad tent (christened "The Red Rooster"), and decorated it with white candles.

Work ended early on Christmas Eve. A light snow had fallen, and the bells of nearby Caen were already pealing faintly. The company choir had been practicing for days. In the evening, prisoners removed their rust-brown camp garb and gathered festively in their *Wehrmacht* uniforms, which inexplicably had not yet been confiscated (but it was the last time they would see them), and even wore their medals. After *"Stille Nacht"* and *"O Tannenbaum,"* Staff Sergeant Heinz Schröder, the senior noncom, made a speech, which Roth described in his diary only as "appropriate," around a blazing bonfire of scrap wood. Another sergeant, "Papa" Ernst Zanft, read a poem, *"Deutschland,"* written for the occasion by Roth, and as the fire diminished to embers, they returned to their unheated tents for a moment of silence for fallen comrades, then to sing, joke, and play "skat* and rummy." On a daily POW diet of rice with raisins, doughnuts, sweetened groats, bread, pea soup, meat-and-potatoes stew, and tea, they could only imagine a "German Christmas"—recalled by Roth as "chocolate and Marzipan, gilded nuts, . . . the wafting fragrance of golden, crusty goose, potatoes boiling, steamed red cabbage, red wine, *Schwarzwald* torte and hot black coffee to keep everyone awake." However, they had fermented their

---

*Skat: a three-handed German card game with bidding for contract.

own *Schnaps* with potatoes, sugar, and water, and made a Christmas of it.

The French would muster thousands of Germans in work camps after the war—but not for the many years of forced labor as the Russians did in the East. Mining coal, Roth would spend two further Christmases, and some months beyond, as a prisoner.

Eight miles east of Bande, at a château near La Roche, General von Manteuffel telephoned Hitler's headquarters. "Time is running short," he reminded Alfred Jodl. A reappraisal was in order. The *Führer* had expected them to exploit surprise and reach the Meuse in three days. December 24 was far beyond their expected fuel limits. Manteuffel's left flank was not covered: the salient remained too narrow for a breakout. He expected further attacks now from Patton's troops. "You have to let me know what the *Führer* wants. The time has come for a complete new plan. I can't keep driving toward the Meuse and still take Bastogne."

"The *Führer* won't like this news."

"It's the damn truth. The most we can do is reach the Meuse. We've been delayed too long at Bastogne. . . . Besides, by this time the Allies are sure to be on the other side of the Meuse in strength."

The futile conversation continued, largely about troop reserves that were not there. "Be assured, my dear Manteuffel," Jodl offered, "the *Führer* will be told immediately."

Manteuffel hung up, heard a shell explode in the distance, and walked down into the château cellar. His staff was sitting on the vacant floor waiting for their orders from Hitler.

The *Führer*'s own *Heilige Abend* was surprisingly—if only

minimally—Christmaslike. He had ignored the holiday all his adult life. Naziism was its own creed. A night person, he arose only at eleven. In his bunker in midafternoon he received an encouraging briefing. An advance battalion of the 2nd Panzers was only three miles from Meuse at Celles. But tanker fuel to continue, he was told, was running short. They would have to turn back.

Walking outdoors with his staff, Hitler watched clouds of enemy aircraft, glittering in the low sunlight, flying high and eastward toward German targets. Distressed, his secretary, Christa Schroeder, asked him timidly over their late vegetarian lunch, "*Mein Führer*, we have lost the war—haven't we?" He assured her they had not.

He walked his German Shepherd, Blondi, and at five took a nap. Another call came from Manteuffel and, apparently on Hitler's orders, the general's appeals were rejected. He was ordered back toward Bastogne. Rundstedt came by to plead in person for his "limited solution" eliminating Antwerp as a goal, a strategy which already seemed too late. "When all goes well, people are on top of the world," Hitler conceded, "but when everything starts to go wrong they just fold up and give in."

Christmas Eve at *Adlerhorst* was marked by some shared cognac and customary toasts of *"prosit!"* ("To your health!"). Hitler's attack order for Christmas Day, relayed to Manteuffel and Lüttwitz from Field Marshal Model, was brief. The southern flank required "Displacement of the enemy at Bastogne." Model called sharply for his Fifth Panzer Army to "lance this boil." Although Manteuffel had counted on the 9th Panzer Division to reach "the extended index finger" toward the Meuse at Celles, he realized that all that would be left after Christmas was a fighting withdrawal.

By telephone, Colonel Wolfgang Maucke, commander of

the depleted 115th Regiment of the 15th Panzer Grenadiers, objected cautiously—he was only a colonel—that orders given after dark on Christmas Eve to attack early the next day left him no opportunity for reconnaissance or coordination. Headquarters staff responded with assurances that even so, a surprise attack on Christmas Day offered great advantages. In any case, the orders came from the *Führer*.

As usual, Hitler kept confidants up late in conversations that were largely soliloquies about vanishing dreams. It was nearly four on Christmas morning when he released them, and retired.

10

MIDNIGHT CLEAR

FROM ACROSS THE LINE, RADIOS IN AMERICAN ARMORED vehicles in Luxembourg could pick up German frequencies airing such festive anticipations of the holiday as *"O kommt all ihr Gläub'gen."* The 70th Tank Battalion attached to Colonel Bob Chance's 12th Infantry could tune in while tuning out the war, making it possible, after the early Christmas Eve farewell bash for Tubby Barton, for Hemingway to jeep over for follow-up champagne. Ground action there seemed far off.

The jollity at the 70th was marred by his reunion with the estranged Mrs. Hemingway—correspondent Martha Gellhorn. She was covering Buck Lanham's command. Papa and Lanham occupied the jeep's front seats while Martha nagged from the rear. Fighter-bombers roared about before dark strafing distant German positions, and, occasionally, from the other side, Allied ones. A lone white vapor trail high in the darkening sky looked different. That, Lanham explained, was Hitler's wonder weapon—a V-2 arching toward England.

At Rochefort, in the tongue of the Bulge westward from Bastogne toward Celles, the 335th Infantry of the 84th Division fended off repeated attacks from Panzer Lehr, then, running short in ammunition, withdrew covered by smoke grenades. General Bayerlein's troops moved into the remains of the town, but a ten-hour march and twenty hours of fighting left them too depleted for pursuit. While they dug into Christmas rations which had unexpectedly followed them, a *Panzergrenadier,* using the armored shield of a knocked-out American 76-mm antitank gun as a message board, chalked on it realistically *Aus di Traum*—the dream is over. Panzer Lehr would get no farther.

On Christmas Eve far to the north of the Bastogne pocket, the run toward the Meuse at Liège by *Kampfgruppe Peiper* was unraveling under artillery fire from 155-mm self-propelled guns and from shortages of fuel. The day before, Peiper had radioed in thinly veiled code about his ammunition and gasoline situation, and his need to withdraw, "Almost all our Hermann is gone. We have no Otto. It is just a question of time before we are completely destroyed. Can we break out?"

That night the Germans had tried to supply Peiper's beleaguered force by parachute drop, giving rise to concerns on the American side that chutists had landed. Many missed the mark and landed in 82nd Airborne areas. Metal cylinders about six feet long and eighteen inches in diameter, they appeared in bad light to be descending human figures. Each cylinder had a large metal button which opened the container on ground impact— but most parachutes snagged on the branches of tall trees and even those which found Peiper's troops could not be retrieved. On first seeing them General Gavin thought, "They must have been great for the resupply of the Afrika Corps." (The Libyan desert had few trees.) Attempting to cross the Amblève to relieve Peiper on the only bridge not blown up by the Americans, *Kampfgruppe* Hansen risked sending a 25-ton *Jagdpanzer* across the narrow, unreinforced span at Petit-Spai. It collapsed and the tank settled into the stream.

Many German units were still in killing condition, although their momentum would soon sag. Near the village of Manhay, much to the west of St. Vith and Vielsalm, Jerry Nelson of the 7th Armored sat out an engagement on the morning of Christmas Eve. He no longer had a tank. To conceal the other C Company Shermans, a bulldozer dug a shallow trench to lower their silhouettes. The 45-ton German Mark V monsters had the high ground. All the American efforts accomplished was to expose black soil against the bright snow, creating easy target practice. Several GI crews evacuated their tanks; others gamely, but briefly, stayed. Soon nine Shermans were ablaze and Manhay overrun. The Germans weren't finished yet.

As darkness came, paratroopers of the 517th Regiment of the 82nd Airborne, and the uprooted tank crews, minus most of their rolling stock, withdrew southwest to a command post near the village of Lamormenil. Since power lines were down, and they seemed isolated, they rigged an electric trouble-lamp cord to a functioning tank outside. "We settled in for another long night," recalled Captain Charles La Chausee of the 517th. "It was Christmas Eve and our radio played appropriate music, '*Stille Nacht*' from a German station, as well as other tunes from the BBC." Sergeant Eldon MacDonald slipped in from the command post in Freyneaux, and unfolded a map showing where they were. Everything east and northeast was German. They had no idea "what the rest of the U.S. Army was up to."

The wired-up radio removed from the tank played on, with familiar Christmas carols and the morale-boosting Field

Order No. 2 from Eisenhower to the troops, already twisted by German propaganda into a perverse Christmas message. La Chausee lamented, "The wrong speech at the wrong time in the wrong place." Holed up in the snow they listened to upbeat language that could only have been written in a location vastly more comfortable than their own. "At last," the Supreme Commander declared, "the German has come out of his fortifications to fight in the open. Good luck! Good hunting!" La Chausee wondered whether they were in the same war.

MacDonald chanced going out to his tank and came back with two bottles—scotch and crème de menthe. "It's a helluva mixture," he said. "I was saving it for New Year's Eve. But it looks like we might not be around come New Year's."

According to La Chausee, the few in the hut shared the booze, "becoming pleasantly numb." They fell asleep.

Some GIs in freezing foxholes stayed awake into Christmas. It was too cold to sleep and they were relieved to be alive. Frank Vari huddled in his foxhole, where he was shelled "all night long. I remember Christmas morning when the sun appeared for a while. We were happy to be able to have hot coffee and bread with marmalade." In the Forest of Höfen on the northeastern shoulder of the Bulge, Pfc Warren Wilson, of I Company, 2nd Battalion, 395th Regiment, managed to write a note for his diary, "The fellows are calling up and down the line wishing each other a Merry Christmas. It is a very pretty night with the ground covered with snow."

It was far less merry for many in the 99th Division's 393rd Regiment in a military hospital at Attendorn near Dusseldorf. Pfc Bernard Macay of B Company, with multiple shrapnel wounds, was in a POW ward on the second floor. His buddies reminisced across the aisles about Christmas at home while resenting aloud being zoo animals for the enemy. "We felt pretty blue. All through the day, German officers [had] brought their wives and girl friends to look at us." For safety, the visitors kept their distance. But one GI who had lost part of an arm, dangled the remnant, which "looked like a slab of raw meat" when unbandaged, toward the partying women, who went screaming down the corridor. The other prisoners laughed.

At darkness the hospital staff laid on a Christmas Eve spread for the German wounded on the ground floor. "We could hear the singing and laughter," Macay remembered. "That made us only more homesick." At about eleven that night, to their surprise, a nurse came upstairs and invited those Americans who could walk to join the celebrants. Some did. "It was quite a gala affair. The women wore long, elegant evening gowns. We thought we were being put on display again, but we soon discarded that thought because of their genuine warmth." The war seemed to have vanished if only for a moment in Christmas gaiety masking postponed catastrophe. Most realized that there was no way that the *Wehrmacht* could win, even if the Bulge had delayed defeat.

Would the Americans, the Germans asked, sing "Silent Night" in English? The POWs did. The Germans answered with *"Stille Nacht."* Together they sang *"O Tannenbaum,"* and mingled other carols in German and English. Before they returned to their ward upstairs, the surprised prisoners were offered dessert.

Well past midnight, a messenger for Lieutenant Colonel Peiper awakened panzer Sergeant Karl Wortmann (asleep in his tank, which was without fuel), banging loudly and shouting "Merry Christmas! Merry Christmas!" Puzzled, as there was nothing to be merry about in the chill predawn fog, Wortmann suddenly realized that *"Fröliche Weihnachten!"* was a prearranged code directing Peiper to destroy all his vehicles and prepare to escape eastward. No one was celebrating anything.

The 1st SS Panzer Regiment's forward position at La Gleize, near the Amblève River below Spa and Malmédy, on the northern flank of the Bulge, had become untenable. The hilly town had few cellars, most of them crowded with wounded of both sides. Frost-flecked dead lay in the streets. Peiper had been queried the day before by 6th SS Panzer Army headquarters about extricating his six Tiger tanks stalled near Stavelot without petrol. He had radioed back caustically, "Send them by air to La Gleize." Circumstances had altered greatly since a German tank accompanied by a half-track had driven up and down the area while an English-speaking *Panzergrenadier* shouted lurid promises of warm female companionship for American soldiers who would surrender. There had been no takers.

Peiper had known the day before that he would have to retreat. That afternoon he called for his highest-ranking prisoner, Major Hal McCown of the 30th Division. Since Peiper anticipated a withdrawal on foot, he could not safely take with him his American prisoners, nor even his own wounded. Although he did not raise the subject, he knew he could be called to account for the murders of soldiers and civilians by his troops at Malmédy. He had no desire to shoot more captives. He offered to leave the Americans in the charge of the senior POW below McCown, Captain Bruce Crissinger, and place his own wounded under a German medical officer. If Peiper's plan worked, the Germans would be turned over to the 1st SS Panzer Division in exchange for the Americans.

McCown, a hostage for the trade-off, was promised his release into the American lines.

For what it was worth, McCown was to sign the imposed bargain and leave the document with Captain Crissinger, then withdraw with the 800 survivors of Peiper's 4,000 men, and the 1,800 remaining from a paratroop regiment. "At 0500," McCown recalled, "we heard the first tank blown up and inside of thirty minutes the entire area formerly occupied by Colonel Peiper's command was a sea of fiercely burning vehicles, the work of the small detachment he left behind to complete the destruction of all his equipment."

The column slipped silently through the somnolent American lines in the early morning light. There was little food to share. An officer gave McCown a few pieces of dried biscuit and two gulps of cognac. The regimental surgeon offered him a piece of captured American Charms candy. When frozen branches underfoot cracked sharply, an American sentry was heard challenging, three times, "Halt! Who's there?" Peiper fired a shot after each shout. Still carrying weapons and rucksacks that seemed heavier with each step (even an unloaded rifle weighed about twelve pounds), the long file turned up steep slopes and slogged across small streams and through thick undergrowth, avoiding towns and villages. With dawn, McCown realized that they were crunching through snow more than a foot deep. Pausing for a moment as rays of the rising sun filtered colorfully through the fir branches, Peiper told McCown mockingly, "Major, I promised you the other night I would get you a tree for Christmas. There it is."

Advance elements of the *Kampfgruppe* somehow splashed across the cold, turbulent Salm unseen by McCown, at the tail of the column, and headed southeast to try to make contact with the 1st SS Panzers. Peiper seemed no longer to be with the group. Rest breaks had vanished with him. Repeated warnings that anyone who fell behind would be shot kept the men together, except for some who collapsed, crawled forward on their hands and knees in the late afternoon darkness of Christmas Day, then vanished into the underbrush.

Forty-seven years later, McCown heard from Bob Hall, one of the 150 prisoners left at La Gleize. Captured on December 19, he had been with an ammunition unit in the 30th Division. "I had you count off [the men]," McCown recalled to Hall, "[then I] appointed a first sergeant and platoon sergeants and reminded you that you were all still under the Articles of War. I remember telling you that we would probably be set free as the German captors were cut off from their own lines."

Given an occasional apple or raw potato as they went, the prisoners had a little less to eat than the enemy, who had little enough. When the farmhouse in which Hall's group of "fifteen to twenty" took refuge was set ablaze by American artillery, they were moved to an abandoned stone church and guarded by a lone teenage German rifleman. On the morning of the 24th, the shelling intensified. "I knew they were coming close. Finally, the German soldier put his gun down and our troops got us. When I walked around, I noticed the German who took my pen. I went over to him and took two or three pens from him." A Christmas present from McCown to himself.

The remnants of the 1st SS Panzers, attempting to spring Peiper's men out, had encountered the 505th Parachute Regiment of the 82nd Airborne. About eight hundred of the Germans had seized a bridge over the Salm River before it could be blown up, opening an escape route. Engineers under Major J.C.H. Lee, Jr., son of Eisenhower's high-handed supply services general in Paris, slipped in and detonated the span as Peiper's party crossed. Yet surviving Germans found other crossings, and on the afternoon of the 24th, the 82nd's commander, General Gavin, ordered a tactical withdrawal for better cover and more open fields of fire.

Gavin's troops had fought the SS in Sicily and in Normandy. They grudged relinquishing any acre they had gained, but on order they rigged another bridge for demolition. "About 21:00 on Christmas Eve," Bill Dunfee recalled, "we were all packed up awaiting orders to move out. Fortunately, our machine guns were still dug in, covering the shallows of the Salm to our immediate front. We were lying on our backs, dozing, when all hell broke loose. The Germans came from our rear, shooting and yelling like a bunch of Indians. I didn't have to see them to know who it was; the rapid rate of fire of the German machine guns and the pink tracers told me. They wanted to go home for Christmas, too."

For many in the 1st SS, there would be no other Christmas. Troops in the 505th rose from their foxholes and began firing. "I would guess less than half [of the Germans] made it to the far bank. Our machine guns, being in place and sighted, really chewed them up as they attempted to ford the river. When the smoke cleared away, we realized we were attempting to withdraw through an enemy force that was withdrawing through us." Gavin called it "a novel tactical experience." There still remained an hour and a half until Christmas Day.

Also near the Salm was the 371st Field Artillery of the shattered 99th Division. The men realized happily that there were no clouds in the sky but for the vapor trails of hundreds of American aircraft. Troops waved at the planes, watching them attract German AA fire. Some were shot down, but for the five hours the bombers and fighters were aloft, the 88-mm fire was directed upward rather than at ground troops. When the aircraft vanished, shelling resumed.

Much of the holiday mail in the transatlantic pipeline had happily been beyond official recall. The 371st had looked forward to its Christmas post, but Dick Byers remembered, "The Germans had captured thousands of pounds of our mail and all the normal supply lines were disrupted. By Christmas Eve, we were feeling really low down and depressed without any mail for a week." The farmhouse that a group of them partially occupied was without electricity, and they gathered for consolation on the second floor around a bottle of "terribly oily cognac" and sooty light from a canteen filled with gasoline and a rope wick. A blown-out windowpane was covered with cardboard. A battery of 240-mm heavy howitzers in the field boomed almost in syncopation with the caroling of local children below. Several were the farmer's own; others were orphans he had gathered in. As they sang in their piping soprano voices, Byers heard " 'Silent Night'—BLAMM! 'Holy Night'—BLAMMM' " The farmhouse shook with every blast, and the cardboard in the window kept popping out. Each time someone would replace it.

As most GIs were about to sack in, someone below shouted, improbably, "Mail call!" One of the happy mysteries of existence in a combat zone is how, whatever the red tape, mail somehow catches up with troops. Byers received two boxes from his future wife. Each had a tin of candy corn as packing for a medicine bottle filled with "good whiskey." He shared the fruitcake, candy, and "a taste of the whiskey," and with the rest of the unexpected bourbon got to sleep with the "customary glow" of Christmas Eve.

Ordered from Nancy to Luxembourg City, in fine weather now for flying, Colonel O'Neill came cautiously by jeep. Greeting him, Patton enthused, "Chaplain, you're the most popular man in this headquarters. You sure stand in good with the Lord and the soldiers." He pinned a Bronze Star Medal on O'Neill's uniform jacket. Later in the day, however, Patton had to confess to his diary, "This has been a very bad Christmas Eve. All along our line we have received violent counterattacks, one of which forced . . . the 4th Armored back some miles [from Bastogne] with the loss of ten tanks. This was probably my fault, because I had been insisting on day and night attacks. This is all right on the first or second day of the battle and when we had the enemy surprised, but after that the men get too tired."

By Christmas Eve the 1st and 2nd Battalions of the 318th Infantry, after a six-hour truck ride, arrived behind the tanks to help General Gaffey force his way north. The drive toward Bastogne was not unraveling, but Patton had underestimated the desperate resilience of the enemy. The *Volksgrenadiers* and *Panzergrenadiers* were fighting not for Hitler, but for the homeland.

With Colonel Codman, Patton went to a Candlelight Communion at the chilly Episcopal church in Luxembourg, which huddled in the shadow of an enormous Catholic cathedral. "It was very nice and we sat in the former Kaiser Wilhelm's box." Nearby, in one of the buildings near the Boulevard de la Liberté (earlier in the war Adolf Hitler Strasse) occupied by Bradley's headquarters people, was Lieutenant Colonel Ralph Ingersoll's intelligence unit. A once-and-future newspaperman with a strong social conscience, Ingersoll was throwing a Christmas party for Luxembourger tots. (Forty-four and a former managing editor of *The New Yorker* and a founder of *Life,* he had enlisted as a private after Pearl Harbor.) All the staff had been collecting "luxury rations" for kids' treats, five-cent chocolate bars, Baby Ruth and Oh Henry! chewables, rolls of Life Savers, and packets of sweet biscuits. By Christmas Eve they had "barrels full of the stuff," as well as several Red Cross girls to officiate.

At the last minute the children's party "got itself a little snafu-ed," Ingersoll recalled, "for through some mistake all the 'nice' children in Luxembourg [City] were already signed up for parties of their own. But the church saved the day and at the last moment the orphans from the local asylum were substituted. . . . They came in two's, clutching each other's hands, and were so excited by the tree and the Santa Claus and everything that by the time they got the[ir] presents they were silent and bug-eyed." There was no dearth of somewhat awkward father figures, all but Santa himself in khaki.

The Christmas tree for the party "was not only home-grown but home decorated. It . . . glistened with silver ornaments and snow made from the aluminum counter-radar foil the bombers dropped. The kids got their little bellies full, for there are more 'nice' children in Luxembourg than there are orphans and the rations had been drawn for the greater number. So everyone had all that could be stuffed into her or him. . . ." The setting hardly seemed a mere ten miles from the *Wehrmacht,* but the Germans were uninterested in recovering the city, which would fall anyway if their thrusts to the north were successful. Ingersoll called it "a front row seat in the bandstand."

Bastogne was really front row. Although at the edges its suburbs were fraying, especially in the south and east, McAuliffe now counted on holding on. So did his operations officer, Harry Kinnard. He typed out a headquarters message to be mimeographed and distributed. "What do you think of my composition, Mac?" he asked as he scrolled it up. "It's my

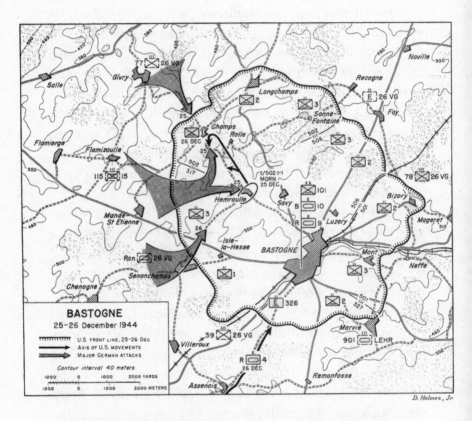

Credit: *United States Army in World War II, The European Theater of Operations, The Ardennes: Battle of the Bulge* By Hugh M. Cole, Office of the Chief of Military History, United States Army, Washington, D.C., 1965

Christmas message to the men." "Mac" was Fred Mackenzie of the Buffalo *Evening News*. Looking for a story, he had been the only correspondent to risk accompanying the Screaming Eagles to Bastogne. Kinnard handed the sheet to him:

Merry Christmas

What's merry about all this, you ask? We're fighting—it's cold—we aren't home. All true, but what has the proud [101st] Eagle Division accomplished with its worthy comrades of the 10th Armored Division, the 705th Tank Destroyer Battalion and all the rest? Just this: We have stopped cold everything that has been thrown at us from the North, South, East and West. . . .

Allied troops are counterattacking in force. We continue to hold Bastogne. By holding Bastogne we assure the success of the Allied Armies. We know that our Division Commander, General Taylor, will say, "Well done!"

We are giving our country and our loved ones at home a worthy Christmas present and [are] being privileged to take part in the gallant feat of arms truly making for ourselves a merry Christmas.

"You should be a writing man," Mackenzie said, diplomatically.

"We'll see what General McAuliffe thinks of it in the morning."

It would be mimeographed and distributed under the general's name on Christmas Eve, with a heading decoration of the division eagle, parachute, paratroop wings, and a "Merry Christmas" ribbon.

The 506th Regiment printed its own news sheet, advertising, with barracks humor, imaginary local Christmas attractions. "The Bastogne Bar and Grill" offered "a tasty luncheon of Ratione de Kay" at the "Café GI, featuring Gerald Kraut and his 88-piece band; [with] Mr. Loofte Waffe and his Flare Dance after sundown." The "Blue Boche" offered the "German War Waltz" by the "Wehrmacht Playboys," who would also perform their hit, "I'm Forever Shouting Kamerad!"

Radioing Troy Middleton at Neufchâteau that evening, McAuliffe confided, "The finest Christmas present the 101st could get would be a relief tomorrow." It was certain not to come from that quarter. Middleton's depleted VIII Corps, with what remained of Major General Norman Cota's 28th Division, was blocked from Bastogne by the Panzer Lehr Division and the 26th *Volksgrenadiers*.

Visiting troops to keep morale up as enemy artillery lobbed shells into Bastogne to keep defenders edgy, McAuliffe heard Christmas carols sung—but in German. He was near the town prison, which held about four hundred POWs. As *Stille Nacht*" faded away, he went inside with an aide to look about, and a prisoner who knew English shouted in holiday mood, "We'll be out of here soon, General, and you'll be in." Another added, "It's nice and cozy in here, General, you'll like it."

Quieting down abruptly, the Germans anticipated a sharp response, but McAuliffe answered, disappointingly, "I just came in to wish you all a Merry Christmas." As he turned to leave, shouts rang out, "Merry Christmas—*Fröhliche Weihnachten!*"

On his way to Bastogne, finally, was Major General Maxwell Taylor, the long-absent commander of the 101st. Canceling his remaining conferences in Washington, he left for France on the

24th, in a freight-carrying C-54. Taylor knew the siege continued, and on landing in Paris on Christmas Day he appealed to
Eisenhower through Beetle Smith to be permitted to parachute
into the town. (Beetle said no.) When Taylor did get back, he
inspected the lines and cautioned troops, "Watch those woods
in front of you!" A GI whispered to another, "What the hell
did he think we were doing while he was in Washington?"

Matthew Ridgway, the intense XVIII Airborne commander
responsible for both the 82nd and the 101st, issued his own
stern Christmas Eve message to commanders on replacing his
equally aggressive replacement, James Gavin. It was nothing
like that of Bernard Law Montgomery, who was only a few
miles away. Surveying his enlarged front with undisguised sat-
isfaction, Monty announced to troops as if he had been in the
fight, "The situation is normal and completely satisfactory.
The enemy has thrown in all his mobile reserves, and this is his
last major offensive effort in this war. This Corps will halt that
effort; then attack and smash him. . . . I want you to reflect that
confidence . . . in all that you say and do."

At seven on Christmas Eve, about a hundred Catholic soldiers
in Bastogne gathered for a Christmas mass in a building where
a large room was converted into a chapel, with candles set in
makeshift tin fixtures on an improvised altar. A young chaplain in vestments celebrated the mass, and soldiers sang carols
accompanied by the padre's portable field organ. From the windows they could see a large building still burning after being
hit by a German bomber flying high and scoring a random hit.
In a brief sermon the chaplain called for further sacrifices and
counseled, "Do not plan, for God's plan will prevail."

Walking out toward his cellar command post, Lieutenant

Colonel Paul Danahy remarked, "Religion is a wonderful thing in a time like this."

"One has some queer sensations," said Fred MacKenzie ambiguously. "At least I do."

As they descended into the cellar, a thin shrieking whistle and the thunder of an explosion shook the corridor. Two more shrieks and blasts followed quickly. Soldiers edged against the walls. Emerging from his Operations Room, Colonel Norman Moore called out, "Steady, men. Keep calm. Don't crowd." Then they heard the fading away of German bombers.

Also in Bastogne, Rifleman Louis Simpson, twenty-one, with a Purple Heart for "losing a bit of skin" (so he wrote home), learned that his forward platoon "could take turns" going to the rear for religious services. "Remembering I was a Christian,"* he wrote wryly in his diary, "I joined the procession of devout men on the path back to Bastogne." The chaplain was conducting what seemed to be a series of masses in the open. "Tonight at home," he told the GIs," our families are praying for us. They are putting presents under the tree and having Christmas dinner. Now, more than ever, here in the Ardennes forest, you feel how much you are missing and the terrible discomfort and danger to which you are exposed. It is for your parents, brothers and sisters, and for the divine history of the birth of Christ, that you are fighting. Those who are attacking you are the enemies of Christ. It may seem strange to you to kill men, but. . . ."

Simpson arose abruptly and "with a sinking heart" returned to his foxhole. He deplored the insensitivity of being reminded "of another life" back home and of "their predicament." If you

---

*As was his father; Simpson's mother (the parents had separated) was Jewish.

don't get prompted regularly about being "in a disaster," he thought, you can fool yourself a little and think your fears are exaggerated. "The chaplain is a good man. It must be difficult for him to reconcile his faith with his occupation."

A photo—it could be anywhere on the Allied side of the Bulge—shows, possibly, Simpson's experience of Christmas Eve. A priest in white vestments over his uniform is presiding at a daylight Christmas mass using the hood of a jeep, covered with a white cloth, as an altar. An enlisted man kneels behind him. The GI audience of about fifty stands under snow-laden branches.

In the sixteenth-century Château Rolle, to the southeast in Champs, where the command post of the 502nd Parachute Infantry Regiment had been set up, the headquarters staff heard Christmas Eve mass in the Rolle chapel, reputedly a tenth-century survival. As only sporadic shelling occurred, the perimeter there was considered "quiet." At midnight, as if the situation were almost normal, McAuliffe jeeped, with lights out in the bright moonlight, to another perimeter village, Savy, a small cluster of buildings, for mass at the command post of the 321st Glider Field Artillery Battalion, a solid stone house. In Abbé Musty's abandoned seminary, where canvas covered the broken stained-glass windows and snow drifted in, soldiers stood in the vaulted chapel to sing "O Little Town of Bethlehem" and "Silent Night." The chapel and transept had become a makeshift auxiliary hospital, and the wounded, some wrapped in brightly colored parachutes from the supply drops, lay on the floors, listening.

Not all the casualties in the Bulge were soldiers. To the north at Malmédy, an American army truck parked at the civilian hospital loaded with Red Cross Christmas packages intended for the troops that were being given to patients who had survived the second "friendly fire" bombing in two days by the Ninth Air Force. An officer and four enlisted men carried in the parcels, and children clapped their hands. The nursing sister offered thanks in German and French.

In Germany, in an old castle now a prison, Red Cross packages were distributed to American POW officers lined up with Colonel George Descheneaux, Jr., at their head. As commander of the 422nd Regiment of the 106th Division, he was the senior prisoner. "Because I ordered you from Limburg," the prison commandant claimed to them, "you men were spared from yesterday's terror raid by your air force. The building you left was hit. Fifty American officers were killed by Allied bombs." The Americans had no means of verifying the toll. A German bugler came in to play taps to remember the prisoner dead. Red Cross food packages were distributed, each a small hoard of corned beef, pâté, salmon, Spam, biscuits, raisins, chocolate, and cheese. To further mark Christmas Day, Descheneaux read aloud a few passages from his Bible.

Less fortunate was Lieutenant Alan Jones, Jr., of the 423rd Regiment, although he had acquired a French overcoat and cap. The small window bars in his crowded boxcar were covered with ice. The fifty occupants included an air force pilot trapped in the Ardennes because he had gone to visit his brother, and who at least had kept his fur-collared flight jacket. "Captured as a damned infantryman," he muttered. They had no idea of time. Suddenly a drone overhead sounded familiar to him. American planes. Bombs hurtled down and the boxcar shook. "Let's sing," someone suggested, inappropriately, and they began, with little enthusiasm, "Jingle Bells." When explosions came nearer, the singing stopped and someone else quavered, "Let's pray." They could hear the thump of a bomb impacting close to the train. That it was a mere thump meant it was only a dud.

In another dim boxcar, Private George Zak recalled, a prisoner he could not see began singing, in a splendid voice, "Silent Night." Others took it up, even sentries on the train platform. As darkness fell on Christmas Eve, an RAF raid prompted the railway guards to flee, and an inmate managed to remove a wire fixing the boxcar door shut. Other POWs worked open the wires to adjoining boxcars, and they piled into a nearby ditch. Bombs fell; some men did not make it. After an all-clear sounded, the guards returned and rounded up the remaining prisoners, who filed in silence into their boxcars. "Hey," a soldier in Zak's car called out once the doors were locked shut, "hey, tenor, give us some more."

From the other end of the car a voice faltered, "He ain't here. He got killed."

Another POW from the 106th Division was Private First Class Kurt Vonnegut, captured with four of his buddies "in a gully about as deep as a World War I trench." Germans in white camouflage suits flushed them out with a loudspeaker blaring that their situation was hopeless. "OK," the GIs conceded. The war was over for them, said the Germans. They were lucky. "We could now be sure we would live through the war, which was more than *they* could be sure of." The prisoners were shipped all the way to Dresden in filthy boxcars, a journey without time. "British mosquito bombers attacked us at night. . . . They hit a car containing most of the officers from our battalion. Every time I say that I hate officers . . . I have to remind myself that practically none of the officers I served with survived. Christmas was in there somewhere."

The only illumination came through the boxcar's vents. Men who crowded around them did not see a bomber drop a flare to expose the target area but they saw the burst, and watched the sky light up—"like it was Christmas."

In Dresden, Vonnegut's squad was put to work two levels underground in "a cement-block hog barn." In the depths of the "meat locker" they survived the catastrophic bombing of the city on February 13, 1945. Twenty-five years later the firestorm became the focus of his half-fantasy novel *Slaughterhouse Five*.

A catastrophe less remembered occurred on Christmas Eve to the Belgian transport *Léopoldville*. The converted cruise ship, built to accommodate 360 passengers, was headed toward Le Havre packed with 2,223 66th Division replacements. Its crew of 237 and its captain were Belgian and Congolese, as befit the ship's name.* The other officers were English. Boarding the dilapidated *Léopoldville,* Private Leo Zarnosky remarked to a buddy, "What a helluva-looking boat. I don't think we'll make it across. Let's swim."

On deck as the overburdened vessel struggled through the cold, rough Channel, Sergeant Franklin Anderson and about a hundred and fifty companions tried to raise spirits by singing Christmas carols Then a German torpedo hit amidships. An Abandon Ship order was broadcast on the intercom—but only in Flemish. In the darkness the crew and its officers fled the sinking hulk, taking the few lifeboats. Although almost two-thirds of the soldiers made it to an accompanying destroyer, others were crushed or drowned as the two ships were pounded into each other by powerful Channel waves. There were 802 GIs lost, but not one crewman.

In an army hospital in the Paris suburb of St. Cloud, Pfc George W. Neill of the ill-fated 395th Regiment of the 99th

---

*Léopoldville in the former Belgian Congo is now Kinshasa.

Division, evacuated via Liège with a battered right leg, had a good Christmas. He would keep his leg; his ward rang with carols sung by a group of WACs; the Red Cross left loaded stockings on all the beds; and patients were served all the traditional holiday trimmings. But a nurse came by with news that some survivors of a disaster off the French coast had arrived at the hospital. She did not know any details. For decades, few would.

The tragedy was covered up. Not until 1959 was a sanitized American report released. A British Admiralty excuse for an inquiry in the 1960s exonerated the crew and officers. A Belgian report in 1992 praised the performance of the cowardly crew and claimed falsely that the lifeboats carried rescued Americans. One who saved himself, Private George Baker, observed years later, "That Christmas Eve, when I, with so many others, jumped into the sea, filled with oh so many boys crying out to God and Mother, is just something that I do not want to recall." The chilled survivors spent Christmas in hospitals from Cherbourg to Paris.

In what had become a backwater of the war, British Captain Nigel Nicolson was with his battery at Fontanelice in the Santerno Valley, north of Florence. On Christmas Eve he heard the Germans ringing the church bells in the hilly frontline village of Imola. "*Stille Nacht, heilige Nacht*" floated down over the snow. Nicolson asked his commanding officer if they could cease firing to listen. Instead, he "ordered our battery to fire a salvo at the church to stop this nonsense. I was incensed."

An impromptu Christmas truce had occurred in December 1914, in Flanders, which became the stuff of legend. As Private Philip Stark, just outside the Belgian village of Verdenne on the northern flank of the Bulge, heard carols carried across the lines in "the clear cold air" of Christmas Eve, he thought of the almost mythic episode, unlikely ever to reoccur. Stark told his buddy, "Wib." As they worked the frozen ground to dig foxholes, he recalled, "We longed for [such] a lull, for a day of peace and safety." Instead, they took a German barrage. "Wib" was killed; a German bullet ricocheted off Stark's machine gun, blinding him in his left eye.

When President Roosevelt addressed the nation and the armed forces on Christmas Eve by radio from his home in Hyde Park, on the Hudson, it was already Christmas Day on the icy banks of the Sambre, the Schelde, the Salm, the Meuse, the Ourthe, the Roer, and the Rhine. It was "not easy" to wish a Merry Christmas, he conceded, to men "at their battle-stations all over the world—or to our allies who fight by their side." Still, the president claimed hopefully, "the Christmas spirit lives tonight in the bitter cold of the front lines in Europe and in the heat of the jungles and swamps of Burma and the Pacific Islands." He waxed unusually sanctimonious not only in asking for Divine protection for "our gallant men and women in the uniforms of the United Nations" but—perhaps with a deliberate vagueness of pronouns—"that He will receive into His infinite grace those who make their supreme sacrifice in the cause of righteousness, in the cause of the love of Him and His teachings." Roosevelt may have been contemplating his own wartime mortality. He knew he was physically failing, although perhaps unaware how precarious his hold on life really was. Most GIs had never known another president. He had been in office for nearly twelve years. When Roosevelt died of a cerebral hemorrhage on April 12, 1945, the end of the war in Europe was twenty-six days away.

11

CHRISTMAS DAY

I N WHAT HAD BECOME A COMMON OCCURRENCE IN the Bulge, although this was on Christmas morning, Private Donald Chumley, assigned to the 90th Division, arrived as a replacement. "I was nineteen, just out of high school—a farm boy with little experience in anything." He was escorted to a vacated foxhole and told to get in and look out for Germans. He didn't catch his sergeant's name. He had no idea who was to his right or his left and couldn't see them anyway. He didn't know what squad, platoon, company, or battalion he belonged to.

Near the Salm, Major McCown's interlude with the *Kampfgruppe Peiper* was nearing an end. Conceding that his men could stumble little farther toward safety, the German captain in charge sent word down the column that they would hole up in the next village they approached rather than detour round it. Under a pale white moon at one in the morning on Christmas Day, as they approached a settled area suggesting shelter, they were greeted by flashing tracer bullets. The

Kampfgruppe password for the day was *Weihnachtsgeschenk* (Christmas present), and *Feldwebel* Karl Laun recalled "a surprise parcel" awaited them down the forest road. In the dim light he recognized "the characteristic Yank steel helmets." The footsoldiers were followed by artillerymen with mortars.

As McCown lay prone, commands were shouted back and forth in German and in English. Arising cautiously, he moved at right angles from the direction of the Americans, then, hearing no one following, he rushed toward them, whistling a recognizable American tune as loudly as he could. Soon he heard the heartwarming, "Put your hands behind your head and get your ass out here where I can see you!" It was a chutist from the 82nd Airborne.

Like McCown before he was separated from other GI prisoners, Colonel Hurley Fuller, courtesy of his rank, was the leader of his column of POWs slogging through the snow toward a German enclosure. Weak from hunger, cold, and exhaustion, many GIs had difficulty keeping up the pace. Word was shouted up the line to Fuller that some who had fallen and were unable to get up had been shot. Even some who had paused only to relieve themselves had been bayoneted. Fuller told other officer POWs that he was going to do something about it. Having already been threatened with death for allegedly permitting German prisoners to be shot, he was gambling on the enemy's respect for discipline. He stopped, turned around toward the column, raised both arms and shouted, as if he were in actual command, "Halt! Fall out on the right."

The order was passed down the long column. The German guards looked at each other for instructions, then jabbered excitedly among themselves. Three officers striding ahead began running back. They found Fuller leaning against a snowbank, watching.

Infuriated, the major in charge of the column barked a command in German. Fuller failed to understand it, but an American private came up and translated. "Sir, he says he is going to shoot you."

"Tell him we're exhausted," said Fuller. "Tell him that if he'll let me control the march, we can make better time and maintain better discipline."

As the private translated, the German major registered astonishment and then anger. He shouted at Fuller, waving his arms and emptily flourishing his riding crop, *"Verrückte Amerikaner!"* Then he looked toward the private, said something in apparent disgust, and walked away.

Without translating the German for "crazy," the private told Fuller, "Colonel, he said *you're* in charge!"

"All right, men," Fuller called out, "fall in."

The prisoners were lining up to restart when the major returned with a small but obviously heavy suitcase which he ordered a prisoner to carry. As the march proceeded, Fuller noticed that the suitcase was being passed from prisoner to prisoner, apparently to share the burden. It wound up at the rear of the column.

About an hour later, when Fuller halted the march for another break, an excited guard led a GI carrying the suitcase to the head of the column. The suitcase hung open, empty. The major hurried up to look, shouted angrily, and struck the GI in the face with his riding crop. Fuller grabbed the major's arm and turned toward his interpreter.

"He claims the American soldier stole everything," said the private.

"What was in the suitcase?"

"Cheese and butter."

Fuller laughed. The contents had become curious emergency

rations redistributed among the prisoners. An impromptu Christmas feast.

The irate major's face turned crimson. He tore away from Fuller and raised the riding crop as if to strike him. Then he laughed and kicked the empty *Koffer* into a snowbank. A month later, Hurley Fuller was still marching, now down a road in Poland. He could hear the roar of approaching Russian guns. Soon he would be taking charge again.

Christmas dinners for POWs ranged from the prosaic to the nonexistent. Radio operator James Fort recalled his boxcar's rumbling into a station—he had no idea where—on Christmas morning and seeing, through a corner vent, townspeople dressed for church strolling past bombed-out ruins. He was desperately hungry. The men aboard had been given little to eat since their capture on December 16. On the train platform was a man with a heaping shopping basket. Fort struggled to get his hand through the vent to gesture with a finger on which was his wedding ring. "Gold! It's gold!" he said. Could he exchange it for *Brot*?

The German wrenched off the ring and pushed into the vent a loaf of heavy, dark bread. Fort pulled it apart and shared it with his platoon. Later in the day the boxcar was unlocked and the shivering men were marched out of the railyards to a camp identified as Bad Orb (Stalag IX-B). But the camp, it turned out, could not accommodate them all. Fort and the men in his car were marched back into it and the door locked. The train groaned off.

Although the holiday was not a *Wehrmacht* priority, some German troops improvised an adequate Christmas. Belgians and Luxembourgers were not glad to see them back. They realized that the renewed German presence would be brief and possibly violent. Even had they professed German sympathies under other circumstances, the war was clearly lost for Hitler. Two months earlier in Luxembourg City, retreating Germans assured burghers that they would return by Christmas, and now, when a truckload of prisoners motored through, an observer taunted from the sidewalk, *"Ja!* You said you'd be back for Christmas!"

Where the Germans had come back as occupiers, a half-destroyed village north of Bastogne opened its remaining shops rather than have them broken into, and Private Herbert Meier, a teenage radioman in a panzer unit, bought a Christmas card intended—somehow—for his parents in Bavaria. His squad was living in a cellar, where it determined to have a party. In a nearby wood, Meier cut down a small tree to decorate. To start, the soldiers brewed captured American coffee, to which they added *Schnaps*. While they drank, Private Meier, the most junior in rank, stood guard in the "ice cold weather."

Southwest of Bastogne, in reoccupied Sibret, Father Georges was celebrating Mass in a cellar when a German chaplain entered and asked to share the space with his grenadiers. The villagers duly made room for the Germans, and after the service, as the troops were leaving, the two priests embraced.

In many occupied villages the Germans insisted on a "sharing" that was closer to expropriating. They ordered local men to cut down nearby evergreens, which they decorated with figures cut from empty cans and cardboard. Women were ordered to bake pies with fruit preserves from their cellars. Musical instruments were extricated from packs, and the grenadiers not in the fighting also fortified themselves with *Schnaps* brought with them, or looted some, and sang carols drunkenly into the night. At one farmhouse, drink turned the troops maudlin.

Teenage Denise Crouquet watched soldiers take family photos from their pockets and turn away to hide their tears. In Bras, west of Sibret, Major General Heinz Kolkott of the 26th *Volksgrenadiers* summoned local children, some refugees from Bastogne, and presented them with chocolate and biscuits retrieved from parachuted American containers that had fallen short. Employing his 77th Regiment of the 26th *Volksgrenadiers* and the 115th Regiment of the 15th *Panzergrenadiers,* Kolkott had already ordered the interruption of the 101st Airborne's Christmas, the attack to come at the western perimeter village of Champs.

At 5:30 a.m. panzers with troops atop them rumbled literally over two unseen companies of the 1st Battalion of the 327th Glider Regiment. Most GIs were deep in foxholes when their empty command post was overrun. Once the tanks had passed over them in the dim predawn light, the chutists emerged and pursued the surprised Germans from their rear.

A German radio message had reported their panzers at the edge of Bastogne itself. Then there was silence. Colonel Maucke sent out a liaison officer to locate them but he failed to return. A column had encountered two companies of the grounded 502nd Glider Infantry. They fired at the white-clad enemy foot-soldiers crouching on the tanks, stripping them off. The tanks veered off course, exposing their vulnerable flanks to fire from a company of the hidden 705th Tank Destroyer Battalion. The second German column was attacked by a company of the 502nd Glider Infantry. One tank was captured intact, seventeen others were wrecked.

As the surviving tanks clanked on, lightened by the loss of their outriders, they were hit by cross fire from four more tank destroyers, bazooka fire from a battalion of the 463rd Para-chute Field Artillery Battalion, and tanks from Team Roberts. By noon on Christmas Day, after hours of puzzling radio silence, Colonel Maucke himself went forward toward Champs with a search squad but was driven back by machine-gun fire. Withdrawing, he gathered the remnants of his battalion west of Bastogne, where American fighter-bombers blasted them. In the early afternoon, before darkness set in, General Kolkott called off further attacks, hoping to regroup and try again under cover of Christmas night.

Near Bastogne, Corporal John L. Hill, a lanky former ASTP engineering student now a battalion radioman with the green, unproven 491st Armored Field Artillery, was "pointed at a crossroads to direct the column down the correct road. . . . A German airplane flew over and strafed the village nearby. Since I spoke French, I was an immediate hit with the civilians in the area. They brought me a bottle of wine. . . . By the time the column arrived I was feeling no pain. Thankfully I was still able to direct the column down the correct way." He learned quickly to listen for two distinct sounds—that of an incoming .88 shell (the instant of reaction time was only enough to warn of the next round) and the Morse signal change of three letters that came at midnight. His outfit, heading toward Juseret, south of Bastogne, and 103 miles from where they began, sang carols in the cold. According to the battery's mimeographed history, "Many men who had forgotten how to pray, suddenly remembered that night."

Hill's Christmas present from the enemy came a few days late. Happily for his musical bent, he picked up a violin in its case abandoned by a German. Taking off his gloves despite the bitter weather, he undid the latches and passed the bow over its strings. The chords clashed with the clanking of armor treads, but the instrument seemed in working condition. Hill carried it off and played it for years after the war.

When Monsieur Schmitz, the village schoolmaster at Champs, returned from Bastogne after Christmas to his devastated classroom, he found an agonized message chalked (in German) on his undamaged blackboard:

> May the world never again live through such a Christmas night! Nothing is more horrible than meeting one's fate, far from mother, wife, and children.
>
> Is it worthy of man's destiny to bereave a mother of her son, a wife of her husband, or children of their father?
>
> Life was bequeathed to us in order that we might love and be considerate to one another.
>
> From the ruins, out of blood and death shall come forth a brotherly world.
>
> —*A German officer*

That Christmas morning, Patton had noted in his diary, "A clear, cold Christmas, lovely weather for killing Germans, which seems a bit queer, seeing Whose birthday it is." He spent much of his day visiting, in the sharp frost, units of several of his divisions to ensure that his orders that every soldier in the Third Army where possible have a hot turkey dinner on Christmas Day were carried out. (For most it would be welcome but less than festive hot turkey sandwiches with gravy.) Boisterous and noisy to stir enthusiasm, he turned up helmeted but unescorted, driven by Sergeant Mims in an open jeep with extra mud flaps, Plexiglas doors, and a thirty-caliber machine gun mounted on a post. "He'd stop and talk to the troops,"

Mims recalled, "ask them, did they get turkey, how was it, and all that." On one inspection, Patton stumbled over the feet of a GI who was zonked out under his jeep. "Goddam it!" the groggy soldier complained. "Can't you see I'm sleeping?"

"At least one person around here knows what he's doing," cracked the general, unseen from below.

When Patton caught up with a column of the 4th Armored, still short of Bastogne, trucks and tanks were sliding off the icy road—he called it a bowling alley—into ditches. "I only saw him once," a GI told Beatrice Patton after the war. "We were stuck in the snow and he come by in a jeep. His face was awful red and he must have been about froze riding in that open jeep. He yelled to us to get out and push, and first I knew, there was General Patton pushing right alongside of me. . . . He never asked a man to do what he wouldn't do himself."

As Patton neared the headquarters unit of the 4th, an American plane strafed the area. He threw off his lap blanket and huddled in another ditch.

Several days later, arriving in Bastogne with Marlene Dietrich, he saw white-clad enemy bodies frozen in the snow where they had fallen, now with a second coating of white. "Finest battlefield I ever saw," said Patton.

Also on Christmas morning, without waiting for authorization from Montgomery, Major General J. Lawton Collins sent Ernest N. Harmon's 2nd Armored Division, with the British 29th Armoured Brigade, a rare UK unit in the fight, to engage the 2nd Panzer Division near the Meuse at Celles, the exposed tip of the Bulge. "The bastards are in the bag," General Harmon reported to Collins. Capture of thirteen German self-propelled guns abandoned for lack of fuel suggested further that the panzers had gone as far west as they could go. Intelligence had already picked up an anxious message from 2nd

Panzer Division headquarters asking whether any fuel supplies had been captured, which Monty on the northern flank interpreted confidently as "the handwriting on the wall."

Realizing from Manteuffel the hopeless situation at Celles, General Jodl at the distant *Adlerhorst* again appealed cautiously, realizing that he faced a rebuff, *"Mein Führer,* we must face the facts. We cannot force the Meuse."

"We have had unexpected setbacks," Hitler acknowledged sourly, "because my plan was not followed to the letter, but all is not lost. The war cannot last as long again as it has already lasted. Nobody could stand it, neither we nor the others." In his tortured reasoning, he explained, "The question is, which side will crack first? I say that the side which lasts longer will do so only if it stands to lose everything. We stand to lose everything. If the other side announces one day, 'We've had enough!' no harm will come to them. If America says, 'Cut! Stop! No more American boys to Europe!' it won't hurt them. New York remains New York. . . . Nothing changes. But if we say, 'We've had enough, we're packing up'—then Germany will cease to exist."

The term he used to his commanders to characterize the grim future of the *Reich* was *"Vernichtung"*—annihilation. The end of the German "race." Only a *"Bereinigung"*—a readjustment—of the perilous situation in the West could permit Germany to focus on repelling Bolshevism in the East. "I have never in my life come to know the term capitulation, and I am one of the men who have worked themselves up from nothing. For me, then, the situation that we find ourselves in is nothing new. The situation was for me at one time a quite different one, and much worse. I'm telling you this only so that you can judge why I pursue my goal with such fanaticism and why nothing can wear me down."

Hitler's self-delusion contained some truth. There was no shortage of desire, or of effort, in his increasingly makeshift armies in the Bulge as long as Germans realized that it was their last effort in the West to keep the enemy from their soil. The next frontier was the Rhine. They improvised boldly, stubbornly, often recklessly.

Patton's 328th Infantry had to get past Eschdorf, southeast of Bastogne, to break the vise around the town in its sector. The first Christmas Day assault began at one in the morning, but was stalled by German machine-gun cross fire. Another attempt was called for four o'clock. German guns kept firing into the night.

In the darkness near Eschdorf, Sergeant Egger jogged up and down on the road to keep warm. Several men in his squad desperately wanted to lie down in the snow and sleep, but Egger prodded them to get up. All the battalion's companies had been assigned objectives in and around Eschdorf, but E and F Companies, Egger wrote, "found the town and adjacent area teeming with German infantry and tanks and a lot of their men"—about half—"were taken prisoner, wounded and killed."

By daylight the Germans had covered Eschdorf with machine-gun fire, preventing the Americans from withdrawing. Egger's G Company tried to break into the town from a hill to the west of the road. "In our brown overcoats against the white snow we made perfect targets . . . and were immediately pinned down." Unarmed medics with visible Red Cross armbands made especially good targets. One medic was killed, another wounded. The too-familiar cry of "Mother! Mother! Help me!" came from a GI who cried as he struggled to rise.

"Another burst from the machine gun silenced him. That beseeching plea on that clear, cold Christmas morning will remain with me the rest of my life."

Private Louis Simpson recalled the battle in Bastogne in one of the many poems he would write over a distinguished career. His last line conveys a startling horror:

> *At dawn the first shell landed with a crack.*
> *Then shells and bullets swept the icy woods.*
> *This lasted many days. The snow was black.*
> *The corpses stiffened in their scarlet hoods.*

To his mother he had written, blandly, "I hope you have a happy Christmas, wherever you are. I wish I could be with you. But next time, perhaps."

G Company near Eschdorf had moved up to provide support for E and F Companies, which had run into what Lee Otts called a "buzzsaw." Trapped, troops lay prone in a frozen ditch for six and a half hours. Otts crawled up and down among the men on his hands and knees while bullets zinged above them, trying to keep the men awake and alive. "As long as we kicked our feet together and flexed our hands and fingers I knew we wouldn't freeze." Several men had to be evacuated later for frostbitten hands and feet and faces. What remained of one platoon of F Company "managed to hide out in a barn for thirty hours."

Otts's friend Captain Swift and thirty men in E Company were pinned down, "except that Swiftie crawled out through machine gun and small arms fire and made it to the rear to bring some tanks back. He found two of them but the one he was riding in heading back to Eschdorf was hit broadside by a round from an 88 and the entire crew killed." Swift was thrown twenty feet but picked himself up uninjured only to watch the other tank vanish. Making his way back into town he found his 3rd Platoon. They holed up in an empty building until they were discovered by the 1st Battalion of the 104th the next morning.

"George Company," Otts's own, "didn't catch as much hell as Easy and Fox, but we spent anything but an enjoyable Christmas Day." Appropriately enough, he took shelter in a stable, to the rear of his platoon. Cautiously, they backed into it. In the darkness he stumbled several times over something in the center, and exclaimed "Pardon me!" because he thought he had stumbled into a sleeping GI. Some of his men said it was a log and they had also been sitting on it. "I turned on my flashlight and discovered it was a dead German, frozen stiff with his mouth open and eyes rolled back. I also noticed there was a 155-mm dud on the other side of the room." At least he hoped it was a dud. "Dead Germans didn't bother us too much until we started thinking about sitting on them."

They set up a perimeter defense for the night and rotated men into the stable to keep warm and to eat their K rations. (The wax coverings of K ration boxes made effective fire-starters.) A fresh battalion of the 104th took Eschdorf the next day. What remained of the 2nd Battalion pulled back into reserve, to regroup in a quiet Luxembourg village to the south and have a belated, and hot, Christmas dinner—"turkey, dehydrated potatoes, gravy, sweet potatoes, and cranberries."

In another stable being used by GIs, rifleman Bert H. Morphis of B Company, 1st Battalion of the 26th Infantry, was just out of the hospital and back on duty. Wounded at Aachen on September 20, he had landed with the 1st Division in Normandy in June, and only rejoined his unit after dark on Christmas Eve. Butgenbach, near the River Warche east of Malmédy, he recalled, "was covered with a thick mantle of snow, silvery white in the moonlight. To top it off there was not a sound of war to be heard. Everything was deathly quiet in the snow." He was on the northern shoulder of the Bulge, just above the fighting that extended southwest to Trois Ponts on the Salm. It was possible there to have Christmas dinner with "turkey and the trimmings. . . . It was great." He ate standing up in a stable built under a farmhouse that was the company command post, with the farmer's cattle looking on." From then on he looked forward to tinned meat and beans. In the numbing cold the ground was frozen so deeply and hard that to dig foxholes they employed quarter-pound blocks of TNT with detonators. Using pickaxes, they cut through the snow and soil to dig a hole, emplaced the explosives, moved away, and set them off. Then they would crawl inside "and finish digging the holes to size" while waiting for the war to restart—or orders to move and blast further foxholes wherever they could push the Bulge back.

Near the River Ourthe at Hotton, northeast of Marche, Rockie Blunt had returned to his Easy Company foxhole at dawn after being treated overnight for a concussion. An 88 shell had burst close by. His ears still rang. He kept his head down and cracked open K rations for breakfast. He kept the box handy to defecate in, then threw it as far into the snow as he could. Soon his neck ached from keeping bent below the rim of the foxhole.

"Hey, Blunt," someone whispered from the next hole.

"What?" he whispered back.

"Merry Christmas."

He hadn't remembered what day it was. "Why bother keeping track of the date, for you had long resigned yourself to the fact you were going to die that day anyway. Of this you were always certain." But he had stashed in his pack a four-inch artificial Christmas tree from home. He dug it out and stuck it in the snow at the lip of his frozen foxhole. Then he extracted some candy bars he had saved, a can of C ration pork and beans, and a small can of fruit cocktail from home, which had come from his sister June with crackers and peanut butter. He shared it with Joe Everett in the next hole and they had a frigid yet festive party. Then Blunt spent the next few hours staring at his miniature Christmas tree and thinking "lonesome, melancholy thoughts" of home. He wondered whether the family had received his wired flowers.

Well over a month later, a Christmas package from home arrived. Blunt was in Bovigny, still in Belgium, but on the road back to retaken St. Vith, and had briefly been a prisoner of war until his SS captors surrendered to tankers of the 5th Armored Division. He was offered a belated hot meal—macaroni and cheese, crusty white bread, pineapple slices in syrup, and coffee sprinkled with powdered milk—"a king's feast." His Christmas mail turned out to be a box with candy, animal crackers, popcorn, fruit in a can, dried meat, a box of Cracker Jack, and chewing gum.

Pfc William Horton had received in his mail a tiny celluloid doll, which came damaged. One of its eyes had been punched out. His buddies named it "Purple Heart Mary." Horton hung it on a nearby tree.

High command did not need as many GI Christmas dinners as anticipated: whatever the official statistics, nearly twenty thousand troops would die in the Bulge or of related causes. Many more thousands had been evacuated to hospitals; close to thirty thousand were prisoners of war in German stockades, almost as many as the *Wehrmacht* had boasted. For many others in battle in the Bulge, K rations at best had to do.

*   *   *

Baron Hasso von Manteuffel's Christmas dinner, at his château near La Roche, was also American K rations. He had another captured packet for his dinner guest, Major Willi Johannmeier, who had arrived in a light plane as a result of the general's telephone call on Christmas Eve to Hitler's headquarters. Manteuffel reviewed the bleak situation for the *Führer*'s adjutant. Bringing up two divisions already elsewhere in the salient meant only juggling the existing resources, he said. "The drive to Antwerp must be abandoned at once." Further Allied divisions might be punished in the unforgiving Ardennes, but a victory of Hitlerian proportions was out of the question.

Johannmeier, who would follow Hitler loyally to the endgame of the Chancellery bunker in April, picked up the telephone and called Jodl, explaining what he had heard. Manteuffel took the receiver. "The *Führer* hasn't made his decision yet," Jodl said.

"But you know a decision has to be made now or it may be too late. What's more, I need immediate replacements."

"I can only give you one more armored division," said Jodl. It was the one he had already offered both to Manteuffel and Lüttwitz. "And remember the *Führer* doesn't want you to move back one foot. Go forward! Not back!"

Manteuffel put the phone down.

At the *Adlerhorst,* Hitler had awakened at noon. He was not pleased by a flying visit from Hermann Göring, who came from "Carinhall," his palatial country lodge northeast of Berlin, resplendent with looted art. Ostensibly the *Reichsmarschall* was there to offer holiday greetings, but actually he wanted to use his presumptive immunity from criticism to argue that the war was lost and that the *Führer* should seek a truce with the West. Hitler would have none of it. Anyone who took such a step, he warned Göring, would be shot.

The *Reichsmarschall* said to himself (so he claimed later), "Let's hope it's all over quickly so I can get out of this lunatic asylum." He flew back to Carinhall just before an issue of the soldiers' propaganda paper *Nachrichten für die Truppe* appeared with a story that a Spanish restauranteur had presented the gormandizing Göring with an enormous Christmas box of caviar. Given what grenadiers in the Ardennes were likely to have had for their holiday meals, the unfortunate publicity might have been another reason to have him shot.*

Later in the day the *Führer*'s staff made some effort at Christmas festivity in the war room, and Hitler struggled to appear cheerful. One observer recalled that "his face was haggard and his voice wavered. . . . His handshake was weak and soft; all his movements were those of a senile man; only his eyes retained their flickering gleam and penetrating look." Because his hand on his usable arm trembled, he required a trusted aide to forge his signature secretly onto official documents. Still, he affected holiday geniality, even to accepting a rare glass of wine as everyone toasted the *Führer* and the tottering Third Reich with artificial optimism.

An SS adjutant recalled, "Supper . . . was quite good." Except for Hitler, a vegetarian, the main course was roast goose. (Private Roth in prison camp could only imagine its

---

*However the *Reichsmarschall* would put one last effort into embarrassing the enemy. In Operation *Bodenplatte*, he exploited gross Allied negligence on the next holiday, New Year's Day 1945, by massive early morning raids on air bases in the Low Countries where three hundred neatly parked fighters and bombers were destroyed by rockets and cannon fire and hundreds more damaged. 277 *Luftwaffe* aircraft were lost to AA-fire, many to friendly fire from worried flak gunners protecting V-2 launch sites. Hitler forbade any repetitions: he could not afford wholesale losses of irreplaceable trained pilots, let alone planes.

aroma.) Also served was *Lebkuchen*—the traditional ginger-bread. "Field Marshal Keitel made a speech, short and sweet, then we all sat around a candlelit Christmas tree for a while before going back to work." The next day the adjutant "ran into" Hitler again, who shook his hand and asked about his family, even recalling his two children. The aide was thrilled. "I could do and sacrifice anything for this man."

The more grim Christmas on the Eastern Front was spent waiting for the guillotine blade of the Red Army to fall. German farmers who hoarded their produce and lived remote from urban bombing targets still lived well. An eighteen-year-old paratrooper, Klaus Salzer, wrote home describing his Christmas dinner with a group of comrades at a farm where they were plied with chicken and pork and roast potatoes. "When you haven't had a lot of food for ages," he confided, "and that sort of feast is put in front of you, it's hard not to stuff yourself. A lot of us were horribly ill the next day as a result." It would be his last Christmas.

The gauleiter of East Prussia, the notorious Eric Koch, who lived lavishly at Gross-Friedrich, a large modern house he had arranged to be built with slave labor in a suburb of Königsberg, still contended, at least publicly, that the "master race" could fend off all adversaries. After ordering posters warning that anyone who fled his home as the Russians closed in would be executed as a traitor, he sent a Christmas message in Hitlerian vein to East Prussian soldiers. "We all know," he wrote, "that this battle—which is a matter of 'To be, or not to be'—must and will give us only one outcome, victory, if we are to preserve our nation, our freedom, our daily bread, our living space and a secure future for our children." Castigating the "bestial" enemy, he closed with "The *Heimat* wishes you a healthy Christmas."

At Wildenhoff, the baroque mansion of Graf von Schwerin, an East Prussian aristocrat who had known of the July plot against Hitler but declined to join it, the family shared Christmas with their household staff and the Russian, Polish, and French prisoners who worked on the estate. Small gifts of wool were distributed, for them to knit clothes for the long winter that remained, should any survive it. They drank toasts in confiscated whiskey, liquors, and champagne from the Wildenhoff cellars bountiful with bottles brought in better times by visiting officers. "We all recognized that we were living on a volcano," Eleonore Burgsdorff, the count's stepdaughter, wrote, having returned from a two-year stint with the Reich Labor Service. "Our Russians knew that, for them, the coming of the Red Army meant death." The prisoners sang carols in the courtyard. Then Graf von Schwerin left with hours of Christmas Day still remaining to command a *Volksturm* unit. Three weeks later he was dead. A week after, Wildenhoff was in flames.

Field Marshal Montgomery had dragged his feet about liberating most of Holland, and the Dutch would experience a winter—and much of the bleak spring following—in severe hunger. Yet it was bliss compared to that of the concentration camp inmates at Amersfoort, northeast of Utrecht. There the German commandant celebrated Christmas by cancelling all food for captives, and ordering an *Appell*—a roll call and inspection—on the frozen parade ground in the snow from seven into the afternoon. To blight their day further, he had the Christmas geese for the guards' festive dinner hung tantalizingly on the barbed wire fence until they were taken down for roasting.

As the 4th Armored pounded north, German shelling from three sides of Bastogne reached from the lowlands at Champs to McAuliffe's headquarters in the town square. Lieutenant Colonel Paul Danahy's situation map marked with red symbols was on an easel in Harry Kinnard's operations room. Scrawled across it in green crayon was "Merry Christmas."

At sundown, six senior headquarters officers keeping warm in field jackets huddled with McAuliffe above the cellar command post of the 101st for a quiet holiday supper somewhat short on holiday decor and trimmings. The table centerpiece was a cluster of clipped spruce branches topped by a paper star. McAuliffe's messman, Master Sergeant Herman Smith, served tinned salmon and K ration biscuits as the main course, with ersatz coffee and—since they had doughnut flour and K rations lemonade packets—a lemon meringue pie.

Many men on the perimeter had only cold white beans and a coagulated cold broth. Those with lemonade packets mixed the powder with snow and made primitive sherbet. Sergeant Forrest Guth, who had jumped into Normandy with E Company of the 506th Parachute Infantry on D-Day, and again into Holland in September, where he was injured and hospitalized in England, was back, and remembered a hot meal in Bastogne on Christmas, although he was far less certain about it sixty years later. Jack Agnew, a radio operator listening for signs of the approaching 4th Armored, had hot C rations ("an improvement over Ks with cow beets and onions"). Unfortunately the only fresh meat available had been squeezed out of a porker by the treads of a tank. It was frozen stiff. "I stuck it up against a tree and it looked like a bread cutting-board."

Reinforcements en route to Patton's Third Army included

a former outfit taken out of the line, the 87th Division, which had crossed the Channel soon after Thanksgiving. Its 346th Regiment had made its first attack on December 11 and was badly mauled. Pulled back, its commander relieved, it was refitted and ordered back by Eisenhower to the Bastogne-Houffalize area. After nine hours on trucks, Private Alan Shapiro's Company E arrived in Reims on Christmas Eve. "We had a complete night's sleep, a wonderful Christmas present. Midway through the morning, many went to Christmas services given by chaplains. We also received a chicken dinner, with fresh vegetables . . . For the first time in many weeks I felt as if I had really eaten." Men of the 346th then stood about "warming fires" until nightfall, when, a platoon per truck, they were crowded in for twelve more hours of "interminable" nonstop jolting eastward. "When we finally stopped and left the trucks, we didn't know where we were or even what country we were in. There were woods all around us. We marched off into them a few hundred yards away and dug in."

But for opportune circumstances, the festive dimension of Christmas was scarce in the Bulge. In its southern flank, close to the German border, Corporal Clair Gadonik, with the 90th Division, occupied at Christmas Eve an abandoned farmhouse. The stove was cold, and his company tried to fire it, but heavy smoke backed up, suggesting a blockage. The chimney proved to be stuffed with smoked hams and sausages that the fleeing German family had hidden. The entire company enjoyed two days of unexpected dinners. In the northern flank a more modest find benefited the Germans. Lieutenant Gottfried Kischkel, driving a tank through a Belgian wood, heard a comrade shout, "Look in the trees!" Like oversized Christmas ornaments, two canned hams labeled "Hormel" were hanging in a net, apparently dropped by an American plane—and not intended for the enemy. Brandishing their find, the panzer crew imposed themselves on a Belgian family, who prepared the hams and added potatoes, fruit salad, and their own apple liquor. At the table their elderly host rose and said, in German, "I am the mayor of this little town. Although our countries are at war, I come from German ancestry, as you can hear from my accent. This feast is a friendly gesture to you, as you are all poor young men so unlucky to find yourselves fighting a war on Christmas Day."

At least one Christmas story of the Bulge which deals with food seems purely mythical. There are no names, places, and units identified. In it a cook with the German army had left his wife and small son in a small house in the woods, seemingly out of harm's way. Three American soldiers unable to locate the rest of their group in the cold and darkness stumble toward the house when they see a light beckoning from a window. Savory smoke streams from its chimney. They knock and ask to come in to get warm.

The *Hausfrau* has a chicken cooking. Although it is hardly sufficient for her son and herself, she invites them to share it. As one of the soldiers hobbles in wounded, she is solicitous about him. The soldiers discover that she speaks French as well as German.

There is another knock on the door. The GIs reach for their guns. Four German soldiers claim to be lost and ask for shelter. "Yes, you can come in for Christmas dinner," she says, "but I have other guests."

"Americans," one German recognizes.

They are Americans, she says, but this is Christmas, and all of them would have to lay down their weapons. There would be no killing on this night. She also instructs the Americans to put away their guns. But the atmosphere is tense. For some minutes the room remains quiet. Breaking the silence, one American offers the Germans cigarettes, at that time a great prize. The Germans accept. Then one of them asks about the wounded American, confides that he has some medical training, and offers to make him more comfortable.

Christmas dinner is now ready, and the small chicken and trimmings, miraculously, somehow, as in familiar folk tales, will feed eight adults and a boy. But before they may begin to share it, the *Hausfrau* makes a little speech. All war is wrong, she says in German and then in French. Christmas is about peace and goodwill. After the meal the soldiers sing "Silent Night," each group in its own language.

There is only the floor, but the soldiers go to sleep under the *Hausfrau*'s roof. In the morning, the Germans construct a crude stretcher from branches in the wood and explain to the Americans how to get back to their lines. Then they offer to take mother and son into the German lines to find her husband.

However saccharine the tale was, it suggested hope in defeat. Families would survive somehow; despite Hitler. Germany, too, would survive.

12

WINDING UP

PATTON ENJOYED HIS CHRISTMAS DINNER AT BRADLEY'S well-stocked mess in the Alfa Hotel in Luxembourg City, where the staff had trimmed a tree with scraps from the tinted window of a downed bomber. His troops grinding toward Bastogne largely got the symbols without the substance—their hot turkey sandwiches smothered in rapidly chilling gravy. He had gotten his wish of good weather, at least briefly, and his troops were executing one of the most effective turnarounds in history. By March they would be at the Rhine, as the Russians pressed from the east, and the *Reich* was collapsing.

Flying north, munching an apple and a pear en route in the reasonable expectation that he would be offered no lunch, Bradley had spent an hour with Montgomery at Zondhoven, near the quiet Dutch border, after landing at St. Trond, the nearest strip. Bradley and Hansen found no one from Monty's command post to meet them on the tarmac. Then a Hodges aide, Captain Bill Sylvan, turned up in a staff car.

As they approached the village from which Montgomery

operated, they saw gaily dressed children. "What's happening?" asked Bradley, leaning out his window.

"It's Christmas, General," said a child who recognized his stars.

A sign read, "All vehicle traffic keep left." Clearly it was Monty territory. Directions to 21st Army Group headquarters led only to a military police station, where a sergeant washing out his mess gear—clearly he had no Christmas—pointed the way to an unobtrusive and unmarked house. In recognition of the holiday—the gesture could not have been for Bradley— Montgomery had removed his trademark brown sweater and wore full uniform, from rows of ribbons to shiny leather boots. Bradley looked, as intended, humiliated and ill at ease.

Montgomery exuded pessimism about when Allied forces could regroup and press toward the Rhine. Although he now had the American First and Ninth Armies as well as his own forces available for a counterattack, he was his usual overcautious self. He asked what Eisenhower proposed to do, as he had heard nothing from Versailles since the shift in command. Bradley claimed he had no idea. He had not seen Eisenhower, still penned in by kidnapping fears, since Verdun and didn't know.

Montgomery had committed few British troops to blunting the Bulge, and viewed affairs largely from his godlike perspective. "I simply can't pass over to the offensive," he told Bradley. "There will be at least one more enemy blow on my flank. When the German has exhausted himself, then I'll attack." As a precaution, however, Montgomery had moved his 30 Corps under General Brian Horrocks behind the Meuse to back up Hodges.

To Phyllis Reynolds, wife of David Montgomery's public school master at Amesbury, and also his guardian, Monty wrote on Christmas Day that his plans for coming home for the holidays had failed to "mature." The Germans "decreed otherwise," he explained. "The Americans have taken a 1st class bloody nose; I have taken over command of the First and Ninth American armies and all troops in the northern part of the front, and I am sorting out the mess. I hope you will all have a very happy time." He never mentioned David.

Intending to be back in Luxembourg City before dark, Bradley bypassed the impotent Hodges, then in Verviers, and flew back in his Piper Cub for dinner with Patton. During the remainder of the Bulge offensive, he saw neither Hodges nor Simpson. At least temporarily, however, he had no responsibility for them.

Montgomery's precise, deliberate manner was a relief to some American generals who wanted reinforcements in place before making anything but defensive adjustments. In his memoirs he claimed—it must have been a minority opinion—that American commanders "seemed delighted to have someone give them firm orders." (One, however, was the diplomatic Joe Collins, who judged Monty's cautious generalship during the weeks of the Bulge "effective Allied cooperation.") He did redeploy Allied troops on the northern shoulder of the Bulge, with some small withdrawals at the start, to forestall the fuel-starved Germans. But, ungraciously as always, Monty announced that he was only there to provide "proper supervision and control." To Field Marshal Alan Brooke in London he reported on Christmas evening that he had been "absolutely frank" with Bradley, whose discomfiture he rubbed in. "Poor chap," Monty reflected, Bradley was "such a decent fellow," but over his head, having never before commanded anything larger than a corps. Also he had mistakenly permitted Patton "to go too far."

Patton's speed and reach were not Montgomery's style. Bradley quoted Monty to Patton as estimating that it would take three months to straighten out the Bulge—and that Monty was the only one capable of renewing the attack although his combined forces were still "too weak" for that. "Personally," Montgomery told his aides, "I am enjoying a very interesting battle . . . I do not see how this is going to turn into what Ike calls 'our greatest victory.'" He was smugly certain that the outcome would be his taking over the ground campaign in the West for the remainder of the war. The Germans, he told Bradley in a term that pleased him (and then repeated to Brooke), had "given us a real bloody nose. It was useless to pretend that we were going to turn this quickly into a great victory and we had much better admit it. . . . The enemy saw his chance and took it."

The *Daily Mail* would berate Bradley in an editorial, "A Slur on Monty," for insisting that Montgomery's new role was temporary and that the Americans placed under him would be reassigned, leaving Monty only his original 21st Army Group. When the emergency was over and Montgomery wouldn't be needed, the *Mail* predicted acidly, he would "again be pushed back into the semi-obscurity that was his lot before the Ardennes. . . ."

Patton's way of war, rather than Monty's, would flatten the Bulge. In his diary, Patton wished that "Ike were more of a gambler, but he is certainly a lion compared to Montgomery, and Bradley is better than Ike as far as nerve is concerned." He downplayed Montgomery as "disgusting," eager to impugn "the valor of our army and the confidence of our people." Patton's Christmas wish was that Eisenhower would not give in weakly to Monty's "tidying up the lines" panaceas. "If ordered to fall back, I think I will ask to be relieved."

Eisenhower's mess on Christmas Day at Versailles set out roast turkey with all the traditional trimmings. His hostess as usual was Kay Summersby of his staff. Ike unwrapped his gifts early, tried on the fancy slippers which Mamie had sent him, and smoked some of the king-sized cigarettes she included, which, he wrote to her, would give him more time "to devote to the job," as he would not have to pause so often to light another. In her diary Lieutenant Summersby noted that "E. is a bit low in his mind" because of unabated worries about kidnapping, and stayed close to his office.

Although the Supreme Commander remained "in confinement" on Christmas Day, as Kay put it—Skorzeny's greatest if unintended achievement—the old Eisenhower would soon emerge. Although delayed by bad weather, he would fly to Brussels to meet with Montgomery, whose vanity did not permit his traveling to Ike. Press criticism of Eisenhower in London remained outspokenly rude, and Marshall and Stimson were furious, as the war of words seemed to them the only current evidence of British pugnacity. It led to an "eyes only" radio message to Eisenhower from Marshall conceding that he was violating his own orders to Pentagon staff about not bothering him "while you are in the turmoil of this German offensive." Still, without mentioning Montgomery by name, Marshall urged Eisenhower to keep his backbone rigid. Articles in "certain London papers" had proposed "a British Deputy Commander for all your ground forces," Marshall wrote, "implying that you have undertaken too much of a task yourself. My feeling is this: under no circumstances make any concessions of any kind whatsoever. You not only have our complete confidence but there would be terrific resentment in this country following such action. I am not assuming that you had in mind such a concession. I just wish you to be certain of our attitude on this side. You are doing a grand job and go on and give them hell."

In the northern shoulder of the Bulge under Montgomery, despite—or because of—his caution, and certainly because of poor roads, poor weather, and paucity of fuel, the intensity of von Rundstedt's offensive had waned. Stability was returning to a very different front than had existed on December 16, hardly ten days before. In a Christmas Day assessment, Rundstedt informed Hitler that even the *Kleine Lösung* (small solution) he had proposed unsuccessfully—to surround and disable divisions threatening the *Heimat*—now seemed thoroughly inoperable. They had no more reserve depth and replacement armor. The best they could do was to withdraw behind the Westwall before their best remaining forces were obliterated. His persuasion was lost on Hitler. However useless, his orders to press on were not rescinded.

Fighting everywhere in the Bulge was as intense on Christmas Day and the next as it had been since the balloon went up. Grenadiers in white capes and sheets, blending in with the snow, fired into doors and windows in villages, and took fire from Americans in foxholes and behind barns. Woods and ravines and riverbanks changed hands, then changed hands again. Although the weather was again turning poor, P-38s and British Typhoons flew multiple sorties, landing only to replenish fuel and fill ammunition racks, and worked over clearings in the woods harboring suspected enemy tanks and trucks.

On Christmas night in the north, the 19th Panzer Grenadier Regiment of the 9th Panzer Division, ordered to break across the Salm River at Vielsalm, again hit the 82nd Airborne's 508th Regiment. After a three-hour firefight, while screaming and yelling in futile attacks, the Germans were beaten back. They would return again until finally stopped for good. Slowly, the Bulge was being pinched and blunted.

In the village of Montjoie, at the command post of the 47th Regiment of the 9th Division, where Oberst von der Heydte, now a POW, was in a clearing hospital, an American officer came to him and asked whether he wanted to confess. He thought, "My goodness, now at the end I shall be shot!" The officer turned out to be a chaplain. He understood that Baron von der Heydte, a Bavarian from an aristocratic family, was a Catholic, and he was being asked, since it was Christmas, "if I wished to confess to take the communion."

Below Bastogne, McAuliffe's artillerymen would frustrate renewed assaults. Kolkott's own 5th Parachute Division and 39th Regiment, now badly mauled, could not close the corridor to the north being forced by Patton's armor. Four miles south of Bastogne on Tuesday morning, December 26, "Second Christmas Day" to the Germans, who had little to celebrate, units of the 4th Armored Division closed in on Bastogne from the southwest. Resistance was still fierce. C-47s making air drops were still drawing antiaircraft fire and taking hits. Kolkott had sought permission on Christmas Day to break off the battle and regroup, which meant withdraw. Higher command—presumably, Hitler—had refused him. Having no other recourse, he withdrew anyway.

The *Zweite Weihnachtstag* afforded an opportunity to Major General Kurt Möhring of the 276th *Volksgrenadier* Division to send a message to his troops hoping that in the inevitable withdrawal behind the *Westwall* they would be able to recapture, however belatedly, the Christmas spirit. All that General Hans Krebs, Model's chief of staff, could do was to concede ambiguously that on Second Christmas Day they had reached "a certain culminating point." Neither concession meant the end of the Bulge, but the air was seeping out of the balloon.

Toward dusk, McAuliffe was informed by radio that the 326th Airborne Engineer Battalion as well as the 37th Tank Battalion, commanded by Lieutenant Colonel Creighton Abrams, were aproaching. McAuliffe jeeped with an aide to see for himself. Other troops followed. At 4:50 p.m. the first tanks threaded through a hastily laid and ineffective German minefield. Fifteen minutes later First Lieutenant Charles P. Boggess of the 37th took his tank, painted boldly next to serial number USA 308308, FIRST IN BASTOGNE, into the American lines. Captain William Dwight came next with his tank, observing with surprise that the 101st command had ensured that its greeting party was well-dressed and clean-shaven.

Some men in the 101st would be indignant at the contention that they had been rescued, for with resupply they had held out on their own. (The division and attached elements would receive a Presidential Unit Citation from Eisenhower, usually awarded to smaller units.) Its casualties through Christmas had been 105 officers and 1,536 men, while the 10th Armored had lost 25 officers and 478 men, but McAuliffe was demonstrating that his division and supporting units had everything under control. Eisenhower would later downplay the armored breakthrough as "only [a] precarious connection with the beleaguered garrison," but it was definitive.

Captain Dwight scrambled from his tank, climbed the hill to McAuliffe's unrelinquished observation post, saluted, and asked, "How are you, General?"

"Gee, I am mighty glad to see you," said McAuliffe, happy to be reconnected. The day *after* Christmas wasn't too bad.

Young Octave Merveille, who had been born in Bastogne, was with his father in Huy, where he was a *Gendarmerie* brigade commander, when the news arrived. He remembered his father talking with American officers over coffee heated on their "steaming hot [potbelly] coal stove" in their snow-covered tents. "I heard the name Patton being mentioned and some kind of happiness lightened their faces as they all were laughing. I felt a sense of relief and I knew that we were, once again, to be saved and free."

AFTERWORD

In reserve after fighting off the Germans in the snow east of the Meuse, men of the 2nd Armored Division sat down in warm billets on December 31 to their belated Christmas dinners. Not until the end of January 1945, six weeks after the breakthrough into the Ardennes, was the salient called "the Bulge" fully flattened and the lost ground recovered. Officially at the time, American casualties totaled 80,987, including 10,276 killed and 23,218 missing, plus prisoners of war and unrecovered dead. It was very likely considerably more, especially in dead and prisoners of war. Losses from the sunken *Léopoldville,* and other indirect and air casualties, were kept off the count. More were still unreported.

Eisenhower would remain "considerably disturbed" by references to "the so-called Battle of the Bulge." From his standpoint, he explained to the new secretary of war, Robert Patterson, just before Christmas the next year, "the German winter offensive of December, 1944, was the outcome of a policy for which I was solely responsible and . . . which, starting from the most meager prospects in the minds of many doubters, ended in complete and unqualified victory." He was "unalterably opposed to making any effort to publicize at this time any story concerning the 'Ardennes Battle' "—his preferred but ignored term—or even of allowing any written explanation to go outside the War Department. "I thoroughly believe," he insisted, "that we should continue to regard the Battle as a mere incident in a large campaign and say nothing whatsoever to anyone's expense in response to casual inquiry from our friends." But his war memoirs three years later conceded "the popular name of 'Battle of the Bulge.'"

With few troops committed to active combat, the British took 1,408 casualties, including 200 dead. The Germans estimated up to 98,024 casualties, excluding air losses, with over 12,000 dead and more than 30,000 missing, including prisoners of war. The actuality was probably very much higher. At least 3,000 Belgian and French civilians also died, and many more thousands injured, a third of them from American air strikes.

The Rhine would not be breached until March 7, when a reconnaissance force of the 9th Armored Division under Brigadier General William M. Hoge captured, intact, the Ludendorff railway bridge at Remagen. Patton's Third Army reached the Rhine the same day but then had to assemble vast quantities of bridging material, reaching the east bank only on March 22. Quickly he telephoned Omar Bradley, urging, "For God's sake tell the world we're across. . . . I want the world to know Third Army made it before Monty."

A hospital ship returned some of the wounded at the Bulge, with other casualties, across the Atlantic from Cherbourg, along with nearly a thousand of the dead whose families wanted their fathers and sons to be buried at home. As it was docking in New York, a soldier aboard assigned to the navy as a pharmacist's mate realized that no military formalities had been arranged, yet grieving families were gathering as the ship tied up. Warren Westerman hurried below decks, came up with his clarinet (he had no trumpet), and played impromptu taps from the fantail.

General Alfred Jodl signed articles of unconditional surrender on May 7, 1945, a week after Hitler's suicide in Berlin. Several of his generals in command at the Bulge died by their own hands, notably Field Marshal Model, two weeks before his *Führer*. Göring committed suicide in his prison cell in October 1946; Keitel and Jodl were hanged after the Nuremberg war criminal trials. A Polish court sentenced the brutal Königsberger Erich Koch to life imprisonment. Acquitted at a war crimes trial, Skorzeny found safety in General Franco's Spain; Peiper was sentenced to hang in a postwar trial but was paroled after a short stay in prison; decades later he was murdered by unforgiving Frenchmen. Sepp Dietrich was convicted for war crimes and sentenced to life imprisonment, but, also released rather quickly on probation. Baron von der Heydte, who had taught at the University of Berlin before the war, became a professor of international law at Würzburg.

By war's end, all of the POWs referred to by name in this narrative had been freed. Major Desobry, taken prisoner at Noville, later had Rue du Général Desobry in the town named for him, while Bastogne renamed its town square Place Général A. C. McAuliffe, for the 101st's acting divisional commander. In 1945 Bradley, Hodges, and Patton received four stars at Eisenhower's behest, and Bradley, despite his weak role in the Bulge, became, in 1950, as chairman of the joint chiefs of staff during the Korean War, the last five-star general.

Critically injured on December 9, 1945, in a postwar staff car collision with an army truck in Germany, Patton would not see another Christmas. He died on December 21, 1945, and was buried in a cemetery in Luxembourg for American dead in the Bulge, 6,000 of them from his Third Army, that Christmas Eve.

SOURCES

GENERAL

Many sources are embedded in the narrative itself and not further cited. The most authoritative historical source about the course of events remains *The Ardennes: Battle of the Bulge* by Hugh M. Cole (Washington, D.C., 1965, 1972), volume 8 in the subseries *The European Theater of Operations of the United States Army in World War II*. This volume and other titles listed below are utilized throughout the narrative. Russell F. Weigley's *Eisenhower's Lieutenants. The Campaigns of France and Germany, 1944–1945* (Bloomington, IN, 1990) reprints the 1981 text. Quotations from Patton throughout, unless otherwise credited, are from *The Patton Papers, 1940–1945*, ed. Martin Blumenson (Boston, 1971), and Carlo D'Este's *Patton: A Genius for War* (New York), 1995. Quotations from Eisenhower throughout, unless otherwise cited, are from *The Papers of Dwight David Eisenhower: The War Years,* Alfred D. Chandler, ed. (Baltimore, 1970).

Quotations from Marshall's letters unless otherwise credited are from *The Papers of George Catlett Marshall,* vol. 5, ed. Larry Bland et al. (Baltimore, 2000). Quotations from Marshall's interviews throughout are from Forrest Pogue, ed., *George C. Marshall. Interviews and Reminiscences* (Lexington, VA, 1991). Other Marshall documentation, drawn from Marshall Foundation archives at VMI, are from Pogue's *Marshall. Organizer of Victory* (New York, 1973) and Leonard Mosley's *Marshall: A Hero for Our Times* (New York,

1982). All quotations from the diaries and letters of Field Marshal Alan Brooke are from *War Diaries, 1939–1945. Field Marshal Lord Alanbrooke,* ed. Alex Danchev and Daniel Todman (Berkeley, CA, 2001); this edition restores material censored from earlier printings, which are unreliable. German graffiti on walls and vehicles is quoted from photographs in Philip Michael Vorwald, *Battle of the Bulge through the Lens,* and Danny S. Parker's *Battle of the Bulge* (see notes to chapter 2). Documents from the United States Army Military Institute files in Carlisle, Pennsylvania, are cited throughout as USAMHI.

The amount of Bulge-related history is immense, and obviously not all targeted to the thrust of this book. Readers interested in going beyond library shelves may wish to know of the Centre for Research and Information on the Battle of the Ardennes in Belgium (users.skynet.be/bulgecriba), from which one may access nearly 40,000 online citations.

PREFACE

For Patton's Christmas prayer, see notes to chapter 8. For details of the 1914 Christmas truce, see S. Weintraub, *Silent Night: The Story of the World War I Christmas Truce* (New York, 2001). For Patton's elegy on his friend Captain Matthew L. English, see the "Aftermath" chapter in S. Weintraub, *A Stillness Heard Round the World: The End of the Great War* (New York & London, 1985).

1. NO PEACE

The *Currahee* of the 506th Regiment of the 101st Airborne Division (compiled by Lt. James Moron in 1945) is quoted in Stephen Ambrose's *Band of Brothers* (New York, 1992). Manteuffel's bridge metaphor is quoted in John S. D. Eisenhower's *The Bitter Woods* (New York, 1969). Dwight Eisenhower's wager with Montgomery is in the Eisenhower *Papers.* The army post exchange decision (only partially effective) to divert and return Christmas mail to the U.S. is in Harry Butcher, *My Three Years with Eisenhower: The Personal*

Diary of Captain Harry C. Butcher, USNR (New York, 1946), also cited in later pages. Cole and Weigley both quote "three trees a day." The code names "Christrose," "Autumn Fog," and others appear in many histories and are cited here from John Toland, *Battle: The Story of the Bulge* (New York, 1959).

Churchill's silent alteration of his cable to Smuts is described by David Reynolds in his *In Command of History: Churchill Fighting and Writing the Second World War* (New York, 2005). Nigel Hamilton, *Monty: The Battles of Field Marshal Bernard Montgomery* (New York, 1997) and others quote Montgomery's reports from Major Bigland on Hodges; Colonel William Sylvan's diary reporting the Hodges evacuation of Spa is in USAMHI, as is that of Colonel Charles C. Patterson. William Desobry's oral history is also in the USAMHI.

David Niven's memoir, also quoted later, is *The Moon's a Balloon* (New York, 1972). Montgomery's plans to return to Britain for Christmas are in Nigel Hamilton. The unnamed 12th SS Panzer Division officer's letter to his sister, December 15, 1944, about a "holy war" is quoted in John Strawson's *The Battle for the Ardennes* (London, 1972).

2. CHRISTMAS GIFTS

The size of General Lee's SOS empire in Paris and that of General Bedell Smith are enumerated by Stephen Ambrose in *Citizen Soldiers. The U.S. Army from the Normandy Beaches to the Bulge to the Surrender of Germany* (New York, 1997). Elise Delé-Dunkel's interrogation appears in many accounts. Here it is drawn from Gerald Astor's *A Blood-Dimmed Tide: The Battle of the Bulge by the Men Who Fought It* (New York, 1992). General James Gavin's memoir is *On to Berlin: Battles of an Airborne Commander, 1943–1946* (New York, 1979). Further Gavin references are to this title. Marlene Dietrich relates her Bulge experiences in *Marlene* (New York, 1989), trans. Salvator Attanasio. What she does not tell is in Donald Spoto, *Blue Angel: The Life of Marlene Dietrich* (New York, 1992). Cpl Gerald Nelson's account is drawn from Astor's *A Blood-Dimmed*

Tide. General Ridgway is cited from his own *Soldier: The Memoirs of Matthew B. Ridgway* [as told to Harold H. Martin] (New York, 1956) and from Clay Blair's *Ridgway's Paratroopers* (Garden City, NY, 1985).

For Adolf Hitler, here and beyond, except where otherwise cited, see Ian Kershaw, *Hitler. 1936–1945: Nemesis* (New York, 2000), and a brief chapter in Danny S. Parker's *Battle of the Bulge: Hitler's Ardennes Offensive* (Conshohocken, PA, 1991). For Otto Skorzeny see Toland, *Battle.* For Douglas MacArthur, see Geoffrey Perret, *Old Soldiers Never Die: The Life of Douglas MacArthur* (New York, 1996). For several Bulge-related references, see Astor (above).

Retired general Peyton C. March was quoted in the *New York Times* on December 28, 1944. He estimated the population of Richmond, Virginia, then at about 200,000.

3. BREAKTHROUGH

For Lt Col Jochen Peiper, see John S. D. Eisenhower, *The Bitter Woods.* For the 101st Airborne Division, see its history by Leonard Rapport and Arthur Northwood, *Rendezvous with Destiny* (Washington, 1948) and Stephen Ambrose, *Band of Brothers: E Company, 506th Regiment, 101st Airborne from Normandy to Hitler's Eagle's Nest* (New York, 1992). Bradley's being told about prisoner "samples" is from his *A Soldier's Story* (New York, 1951), ghostwritten by Chester Hansen. Hansen's own diary and index-card notes taken from Bradley dictation for *A Soldier's Story* are in USAMHI.

That Americans confused German tanker crews with SS troops because both wore black is reported by Max Hastings in *Armageddon: The Battle for Germany, 1944–45* (London, 2004).

4. THE REAL THING

Pvt William J. Shapiro's POW account is from Roger Cohen's "The Lost Soldiers of Stalag IX-B," *New York Times Magazine,* February 27, 2005. The accounts of Colonel Fuller and Major McCown

Sources

appear in Toland's *Battle,* Astor's *Blood-Dimmed Tide,* and numerous other Bulge narratives. Victor Brombert's encounters with General Cota and with cousin Ossia appear in *Trains of Thought,* his memoir (New York, 2002). Phil Hannon's war is described in *Blood-Dimmed Tide,* as is Richard McKee's Christmas dinner of molasses. Russell Weigley writes in *Eisenhower's Lieutenants: The Campaign of France and Germany, 1944–1945* (Bloomington, IN, 1990). Hemingway's involvement is described in Carlos Baker's *Ernest Hemingway: A Life Story* (New York, 1969), Mary Welsh Hemingway's *How It Was* (New York, 1976), and a brief chapter in Parker's *Battle of the Bulge.* Sgt Lou Berrena is quoted from an interview by Chris Rosenblum, "Haunted by the Memories," in the *Centre Daily Times* (PA), December 26, 2004. The SS threat to murder Belgians in possession of American flags is recalled by Octave Merveille (then thirteen) in a letter to me, January 17, 2006. General Parker's bazooka challenge to his 78th Division is quoted in *Roer Rhine Ruhr: The Story of the 310th Infantry Regiment, 78th Infantry Division in the War against Germany, 1942–1945* (Tempelhof, Berlin, 1946). Captain Crane's predicament was related to me by his son Joel on November 2, 2005. General Cota's ordering the 28th Division's Christmas mail burned at Wiltz, Luxembourg, is described by Ambrose in *Citizen Soldiers.*

5. RETREATS

Weigley describes Eisenhower's reluctance, despite desperate infantry shortages, to employ "colored" troops, in *Eisenhower's Lieutenants.* The "bail you out" remark by Patton is from John Eisenhower's *Bitter Woods.* It differs slightly in other accounts. David Niven's confrontation by a sentry is from his *The Moon's a Balloon.* Major Don Boyer's interrogation about Mickey Mouse is from John Toland's *Battle.* The experiences of Lt Willi Engel and Lt Willi Fischer are described by Hastings in *Armageddon,* as is that of Lt Joseph Couri. The German "Hello, Joe" greeting is reported in Astor, *A Blood-Dimmed Tide.* Baron von der Heydte's adventures are reported in *The Bitter Woods* and many other accounts. Secretary Stimson's diary quoted here and elsewhere is the basis of his *On Active Service in Peace and War,* McGeorge Bundy, ed. (New York, 1947).

6. MADHOUSE

Toland in *Battle* describes General Clarke's "arrest" as a German. Clarke's oral history is in the Truman Presidential Library, Independence, MO. Roscoe C. Blunt, Jr.'s memoirs are *Inside the Battle of the Bulge: A Private Comes of Age* (Westport, CT, 1994). The black sentry's comment is from Hansen's notes at the USAMHI. Churchill's letter to Smuts is quoted in Reynolds, *In Command of History* (see above). "How would you like to die for Christmas?" is quoted from the 78th Infantry history, *Roer Rhine Ruhr* (above, chapter 4).

7. TURNING ABOUT

The diaries of Bruce E. Egger and Lee MacMillan Otts, Paul Roley, ed., are *G Company's War* (Tuscaloosa, AL, 1992). I spoke to John MacRae on October 14, 2005. Major William Desobry's oral history is in the USAMHI. All accounts of the Bulge quote from it, or each other.

8. "NUTS!"

Sergeant Bill True's memoir, written with Deryck Tufts True, is *The Cow Spoke French: The Story of Sgt William True, American Paratrooper in World War II* (Bennington, VT, 2002). It reproduces the mimeographed "Merry Christmas" sheet under McAuliffe's signature. Lieutenant Rockhammer's euphoria to his wife on the taking of St. Vith is quoted by Hastings in *Armageddon*. Patton's prayer addressing God as "Sir" appears in several books on the Bulge and on the Internet under Pescatore Foundation, which also cites accounts of the foundation's history as an old people's home. At least one text alters "Sir" to "Lord" and makes other editorial changes, perhaps to soften Patton's brash, idiosyncratic, and perhaps (to some of the faithful) sacrilegious language. The building itself, made famous by the Patton connection, appears on a Luxembourg postage stamp issued in March 1992.

9. "ONE MORE SHOPPING DAY"

The travails of Douglas Davidson, MD, were related to General William H. Duncan, MD, by Davidson's wife and daughter and communicated to me in a letter dated March 27, 2005, with an unpublished typescript narrative of Davidson's service career as edited by W. H. Duncan and S. C. Dearing (1997). A monument at Celles topped by an abandoned German tank marks the farthest advance of German armor. A shaft at Dinant overlooking the Meuse, also dated December 24, 1944, marks the destruction by mine of the jeep and German crew. Stephan L. Roth's *Odyssey Tartlau USA* was privately printed for him by On Time Publications, Macomb, IL, 2001. Father Musty and his doomed students are described by Parker and Toland. Parker also describes Hitler's Christmas in more detail than Ian Kershaw.

10. MIDNIGHT CLEAR

The long cover-up of the *Léopoldville* catastrophe is described in Ambrose, *Citizen Soldiers* (above). For Capt La Chausee, Sgt Eldon McDonald, Sgt Bill Dunfee and artilleryman Dick Byers, see *Blood-Rimmed Tide*. Frank Vari recalled his foxhole Christmas morning in a letter to the editor in the *Wilmington News-Journal* (Delaware), December 11, 2004. Kurt Vonnegut's capture and imprisonment is described by Alex Kershaw in *The Longest Winter* (New York, 2004) and by Vonnegut himself in William Rodney Allen, ed., *Conversations with Kurt Vonnegut* (Jackson, MS, 1988). For Col George Deschenaux as POW, see Toland.

Fred MacKenzie's memoir is *The Men of Bastogne* (New York, 1968). Pvt Philip Stark appears in Ambrose's *Citizen Soldiers,* as do

Pvt George Zak and Pvt Herbert Meier. Pfc Bernard Macay's POW hospital account is from George W. Neill, *Infantry Soldier: Holding the Line at the Battle of the Bulge* (Norman, OK, 2003).

Ralph Ingersoll's Christmas in Luxembourg City is described in his *Top Secret* (New York, 1946). The most complete account of "friendly fire" civilian casualties is in Peter Schrijvers, *The Unknown Dead: Civilians in the Battle of the Bulge* (Lexington, KY, 2005). Some of the details from Nigel Nicolson's account of a Christmas in Italy come from his conversations with SW; others are from his memoir, *Long Life* (London, 2002). Roosevelt's radio address is from Conrad Black, *Franklin Delano Roosevelt: Champion of Freedom* (New York, 2003).

11. CHRISTMAS DAY

Pvt Donald Chumley is quoted from Ambrose, *Citizen Soldiers*. Pfc Bert H. Morphis's experience is described from his memoir in *Hitler's Last Gamble: The Battle of the Bulge* (New York, 1994), by Trevor N. Dupuy, David L. Bongard, and Richard C. Anderson, Jr. Louis Simpson's diary and letters relating to the Bulge are in his *Selected Prose* (New York, 1989). His poem "The Battle" appears, complete, in his *Collected Poems* (New York, 1988). Sgt John L. Hill's account is from his privately printed memoir (2002) and an interview with SW, January 20, 2005. Forrest Guth was interviewed by SW in March 2004. Guth, as well as Jack Agnew, Clair Gadolnik, and Gottfried Kischke are in Ambrose, *Citizen Soldiers*. (On one page Kischke is a lieutenant, on a later page Ambrose calls him a private.) Pfc William Horton and "Purple Heart Mary" appear in *Time,* January 8, 1945.

Schoolmaster Schmitz's return to his classroom at Champs is in Parker. Father Georges and Denise Grouquet appear in Schrijvers, *The Unknown Dead.*

For Graf von Schwerin, Eleonore Burgsdoff, and Erich Koch, see Hastings. The sadistic non-Christmas at the Amersfoort concentration camp is also described by Hastings in *Armageddon*. The rather mystical story, "The Christmas Miracle," claims to be the account of Bill Richer as a boy in 1944. It appears on the Internet as www.holytrinity/newrochelle.org.

12. WINDING UP

Col. Sylvan is quoted from his diary and notes in the USAMHI. Montgomery to his son's caregiver is quoted from Ian Hamilton. Octave Merveille's memory of learning of Patton and Bastogne is from his letter to me of January 17, 2006.

AFTERWORD

The casualty figures, almost certainly underreported then and since, are from Cole. Technicalities about what constitutes a Bulge casualty, such as the *Léopoldville* drownings of replacements in the pipeline, and prisoner-of-war camp deaths, omit many related dead and wounded. The account of the impromptu taps at the hospital ship fantail is from Lee Alkair, son in law of Pharmacist's Mate Warren Westerman, as reported to me by Paul Kennedy, March 28, 2006.

ACKNOWLEDGMENTS

I appreciate the assistance in guidance, information, and resources from Lee Alkair, Michael Birkner, Joel Crane, Robert C. Doyle, William F. Duncan, John S. D. Eisenhower, Robert S. Elegant, Selma W. Epp, Dennis Giangreco, Robert Guinsler, Forrest Guth, John L. Hill, Clifton P. Hyatt, Carie Lee Kennedy, Paul M. Kennedy, Rene C. Klein, Sterling Lord, John MacRae, Octave Merveille, the late Nigel Nicolson, Bruce Nichols, Martin R. Quinn, Shirley Rader, Susan Reighard, Stephan L. Roth, Chris Rosenblum, Harold Segal, Richard L. Sommers, Markus Spiecker, Richard Swain, David Weintraub, Rodelle Weintraub, Warren Westerman, Richard E. Winslow, and Peter Zimmerman.

INDEX

ABOUT THE AUTHOR

Stanley Weintraub is Evan Pugh Professor Emeritus of Arts and Humanities at Pennsylvania State University and an adjunct professor at the University of Delaware. His work has largely been in biography and in military history, a subject that has interested him since his service as an army officer during the Korean War. He lives in Newark, Delaware.